just another story

The following work is based on true events. Some names have been changed to respect the privacy of those affected by these events.

Story and art by Ernesto Saade

Graphic Universe™
An imprint of Lerner Publishing Group, Inc.
241 First Avenue North
Minneapolis, MN 55401 USA

For reading levels and more information, look up this title at www.lernerbooks.com.

Design by Athena Currier.
Main body text set in Dinkle.
Typeface provided by Chank.

Library of Congress Cataloging-in-Publication Data

Names: Saade, Ernesto, author, artist.
Title: Just another story : a graphic migration account / story and art by Ernesto Saade.
Description: Minneapolis, MN : Graphic Universe, (2024) | Audience: Ages 14–18 | Audience: Grades 10–12 | Summary: "When Carlos was nineteen, his mother decided to leave her life in El Salvador. Refusing to let her go without him, Carlos joined the journey north. Together they experienced the risks countless people faces as they migrate" —Provided by publisher.
Identifiers: LCCN 2023012812 (print) | LCCN 2023012813 (ebook) | ISBN 9781728474137 (library binding) | ISBN 9798765623367 (paperback) | ISBN 9798765612873 (epub)
Subjects: CYAC: Graphic novels. | Immigrants—Fiction. | Salvadorans—United States—Fiction. | LCGFT: Graphic novels.
Classification: LCC PZ7.7.S114 Ju 2024 (print) | LCC PZ7.7.S114 (ebook) | DDC 741.5/97284—dc23/eng/20230505

LC record available at https://lccn.loc.gov/2023012812
LC ebook record available at https://lccn.loc.gov/2023012813

Manufactured in the United States of America
1-51986-50526-9/18/2023

just another story

A Graphic Migration Account

Ernesto Saade

Graphic Universe™ • Minneapolis

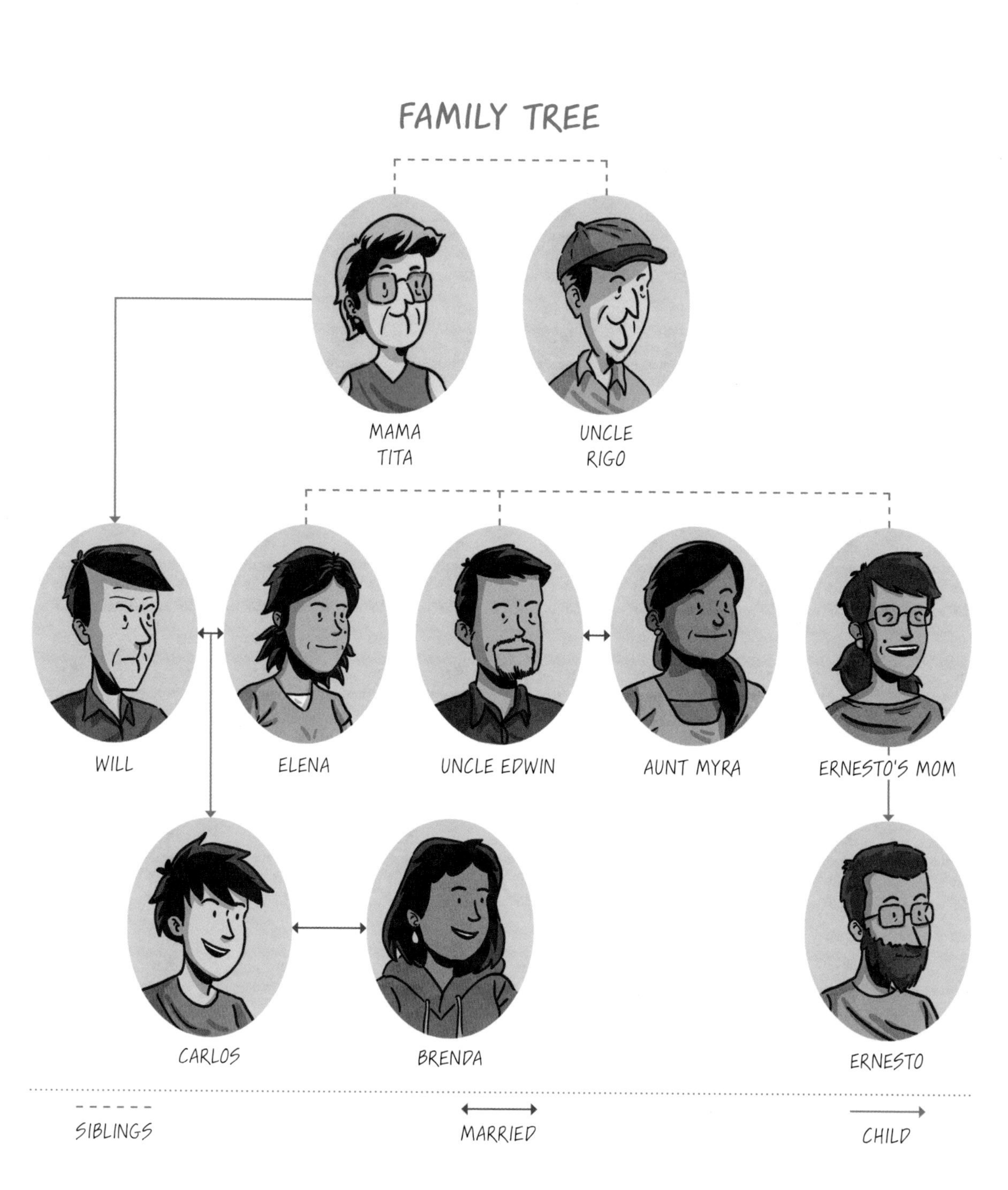
FAMILY TREE
MAMA TITA
UNCLE RIGO
WILL
ELENA
UNCLE EDWIN
AUNT MYRA
ERNESTO'S MOM
CARLOS
BRENDA
ERNESTO
SIBLINGS
MARRIED
CHILD

POFF
SOB
JUST A LITTLE FARTHER...

Chapter 1
10 YEARS LATER

2017
ALL PASSENGERS ON THE AV314 FLIGHT TO LOS ANGELES.
PREPARE TO BOARD.
POLLO CAMPERO
TIA TOYA
MONSEÑOR ÓSCAR ARNULFO ROMERO INTERNATIONAL AIRPORT, EL SALVADOR

FORM.
ZZZ
FORM.
YOUNG MAN. WOULD YOU MIND FILLING OUT MY FORM?
PLEASE.
SURE, SURE, ALL RIGHT. HAND IT TO ME.
YOUR PASSPORT TOO.
PLEASE FILL OUT MINE TOO...
ALL RIGHT. GIVE ME YOUR PASSPORT.
ZZZ
SONNY, COULD YOU FILL OUT MINE TOO?
WHAT A NICE BOY.
*SIGH
COULD YOU ALSO FILL OUT MINE?

Arrivals
Baggage
STAMP
PASSPORT
MR. WONG
LOS ANGELES INTERNATIONAL AIRPORT, UNITED STATES

LOOK, CARLOS. MY MOM SENT YOU THIS.
YEAH! SHE REALLY KNOWS WHAT I LIKE.
OPEN IT UP!
LAX
HOW WAS THE FLIGHT?
I FILLED OUT THE FORMS FOR A BUNCH OF OLD FOLKS.
AGAIN.
CRUNCH
HAH, ERNESTO, YOU'RE SUCH A MAGNET FOR OLD PEOPLE...
MUNCH
I DON'T KNOW WHY, BUT THIS HAPPENS ALL THE TIME!

DURING MY FLIGHT, I WAS THINKING ABOUT YOU AND MY AUNT A LOT.
WHY WAS THAT?
BECAUSE GETTING HERE BY PLANE WAS VERY COMFORTABLE. YOU'RE SITTING THERE, THE FLIGHT GOES FAST, THEY'VE GOT MOVIES SO YOU DON'T GET BORED.
YEAH, SOUNDS NICE.
BESIDES HAVING TO FILL OUT THE FORMS FOR A BUNCH OF OLD FOLKS, THERE ISN'T MUCH TROUBLE.
SO IT GOT ME THINKING HOW HARD IT WAS FOR YOU AND MY AUNT TO COME HERE. I REMEMBER HOW EVERYONE BACK AT HOME WAS SO WORRIED ABOUT YOU GUYS...
IT MADE ME WONDER WHY YOU AND I NEVER TALKED ABOUT IT.
TRUTH BE TOLD, I NEVER SPOKE WITH ANYBODY ABOUT THAT... MAYBE SOME PARTS OF THE STORY, HERE AND THERE.

IT STARTLED ME, KNOWING YOU AND AUNT ELENA WERE LEAVING THE COUNTRY. BUT WE WERE ONLY KIDS—I WASN'T TOTALLY AWARE OF EVERYTHING YOU WERE GOING THROUGH.
NOTHING OUT OF THE ORDINARY. EVERY DAY, THOUSANDS COME TO THE U.S. WITH FAR WORSE STORIES THAN MINE.

I KNOW, BUT NO STORY IS THAT SMALL.

WE'RE STILL FIVE HOURS AWAY FROM THE APARTMENT... I GUESS THIS WOULD BE A GOOD TIME TO GET IT OFF MY CHEST.
YOU SURE?
YEAH, MAN! IT'S BEEN TEN YEARS ALREADY. THE TRAUMA IS ALL GONE...
IT'S JUST THAT I HADN'T HAD THE CHANCE TO TALK ABOUT IT.
I ALWAYS WONDERED WHY YOU GUYS DECIDED TO LEAVE EL SALVADOR.
WELL...

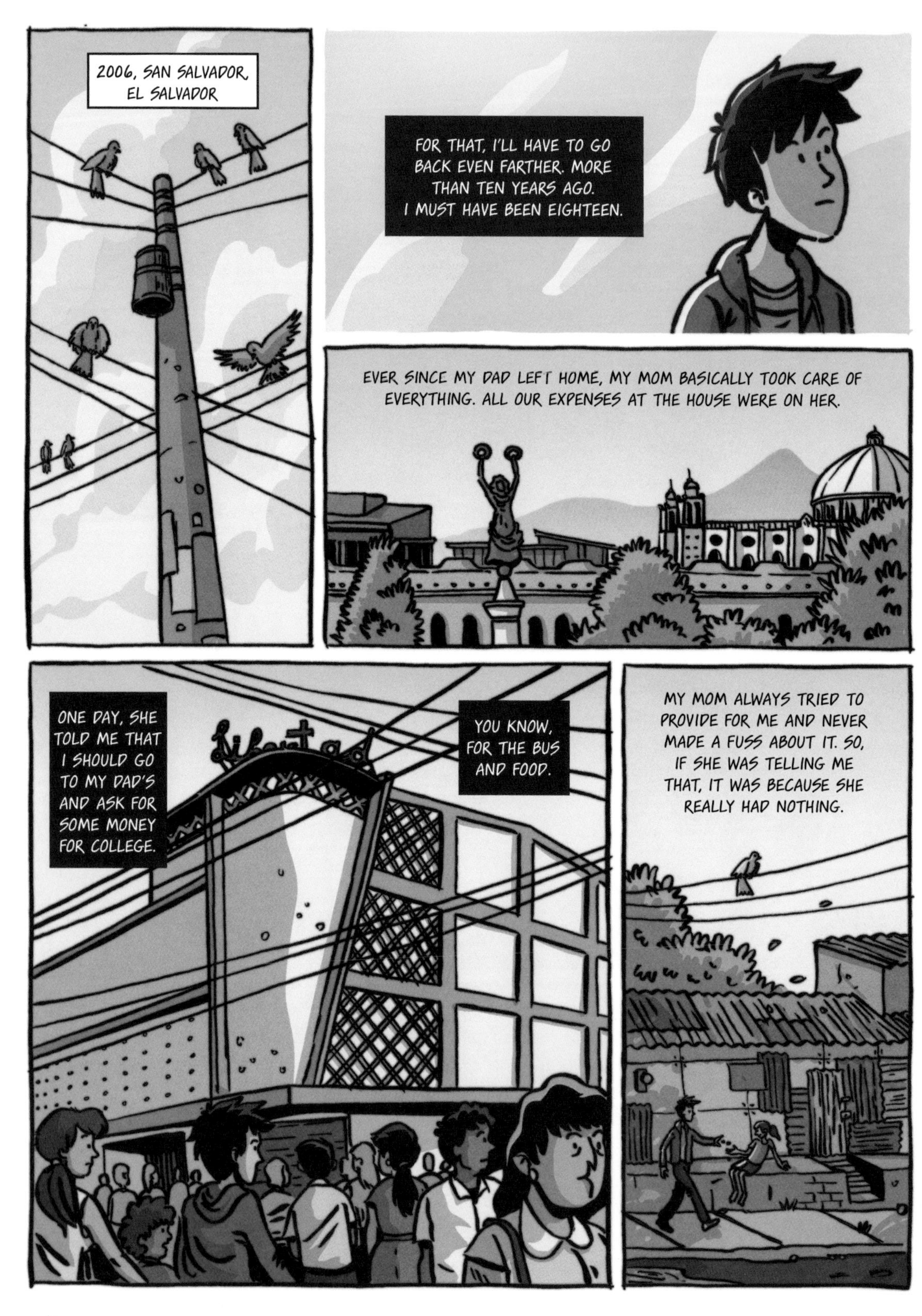
2006, SAN SALVADOR, EL SALVADOR
FOR THAT, I'LL HAVE TO GO BACK EVEN FARTHER. MORE THAN TEN YEARS AGO. I MUST HAVE BEEN EIGHTEEN.
EVER SINCE MY DAD LEFT HOME, MY MOM BASICALLY TOOK CARE OF EVERYTHING. ALL OUR EXPENSES AT THE HOUSE WERE ON HER.
ONE DAY, SHE TOLD ME THAT I SHOULD GO TO MY DAD'S AND ASK FOR SOME MONEY FOR COLLEGE.
YOU KNOW, FOR THE BUS AND FOOD.
MY MOM ALWAYS TRIED TO PROVIDE FOR ME AND NEVER MADE A FUSS ABOUT IT. SO, IF SHE WAS TELLING ME THAT, IT WAS BECAUSE SHE REALLY HAD NOTHING.

HI, CARLITOS.
zzzz
HI, MS. BLANQUI.
YOU SURE HAVE GROWN.
YOUR DAD IS IN THE OFFICE.
SIGH*
HEY, DAD.
SO, WHAT'S GOING ON?
WELL, I JUST WANTED TO ASK YOU FOR SOME MONEY FOR THE WEEK COMING UP...
OH, NO. I DON'T HAVE ANY MONEY.
DAD, HONESTLY, I DON'T HAVE ANYTHING. NOT EVEN BUS FARE.
ALL RIGHT, THEN.
HERE...

JEEZ, DAD, THIS WON'T COVER MORE THAN A SINGLE DAY'S FARE.
YOU WON'T TAKE IT, HUH?
YOU DON'T EVEN CARE, DO YOU?
HOW ABOUT THIS?
MOM HAS BEEN SERIOUSLY THINKING ABOUT LEAVING FOR THE STATES...
AND YOU KNOW WHAT? I'M GOING TOO. IT'S IMPOSSIBLE HERE.
THAT'S NONSENSE. YOU'D JUST GET YOURSELVES KILLED ON THE WAY.
GET A JOB! YOU'LL BE BETTER OFF.

TSSSSSSSSSSS
I ONLY SAID THAT BECAUSE I HAD OVERHEARD MY MOM SAY IT BEFORE, TO CAUSE SOME DRAMA IN FRONT OF MY DAD. HONESTLY, I'D NEVER THOUGHT MUCH ABOUT IT.
THAT WAS MAYBE FIVE OR SIX MONTHS BEFORE THE JOURNEY. BUT MY MOM REALLY HAD FIXED ON THE IDEA OF LEAVING THE COUNTRY, BECAUSE SHE COULDN'T TAKE IT ANYMORE.
YOU KNOW HOW IT WAS. HER JOB WAS TOO MUCH, AND IT WAS HARD TO WORK NIGHTS.
SHE EVEN DID DOUBLE SHIFTS SOMETIMES, JUST TO COVER ALL THE HOUSE EXPENSES AND MY CLASSES.
YEAH... I REMEMBER.
AND THEN YOUR MOM WOULD JUST SLEEP THROUGH HER WHOLE DAY OFF.
THAT'S NOT A LIFE, MAN...
BUT WHAT FINALLY CONVINCED HER TO LEAVE IT ALL BEHIND WAS HER BROTHER, OUR UNCLE EDWIN.
HE TOLD HER THAT OVER HERE, THINGS WERE EASIER, AND YOU COULD QUICKLY GET A GOOD JOB AND MAKE TONS OF MONEY.
UNLIKE IN EL SALVADOR, WHERE SHE BUSTED HER BACK ALL DAY FOR SHITTY PAY.
YOU SAID IT!
CLICK

SO, MY MOM STARTED TO RESEARCH HOW TO COME TO THE U.S.
ONE OF HER COWORKERS HOOKED HER UP WITH A "COYOTE." SOME GUY NAMED GILBERTO.
COME ON, LET'S GO BUY SOMETHING TO DRINK...
CLICK
I'M GONNA PARK OVER HERE.
ell
7-ELEVE
ONE DAY, A MAN CAME TO THE HOUSE TO TALK WITH MOM, THE ONE FROM HER JOB.
IT WAS HIM AND THIS OTHER GUY—GILBERTO. THEY WERE TELLING HER THAT THE JOURNEY WOULD BE EASIER, SAFER, AND FASTER WITH THEM.

*MORE COMMONLY KNOWN AS THE RIO GRANDE IN THE UNITED STATES

MAN... I CAN'T BELIEVE THESE DONUTS!
CHOMP
YOU CAN'T BELIEVE WHAT?
THIS IS RIDICULOUSLY TASTY!!
IT'S JUST A DONUT.
WHATEVER!
SO... WHY DID YOU THINK YOUR MOM WOULDN'T REALLY COME HERE?
I THOUGHT THAT IF, FOR SOME REASON, SHE DID LEAVE EL SALVADOR, SHE WOULD ONLY MAKE IT THROUGH GUATEMALA. THEN SHE WOULD HEAD BACK WHEN SHE REALIZED EVERYTHING THEY'D SAID WAS A LOAD OF CRAP.
ON THE OTHER HAND, THE IDEA OF LIVING ON MY OWN IN SAN SALVADOR WAS VERY APPEALING. I WOULD PICTURE MYSELF HAVING MY FRIENDS OVER FOR PARTIES, NO ONE AROUND TO STOP ME...
ACTUALLY, IT WOULDN'T HAVE BEEN MUCH DIFFERENT. MOM WAS BARELY AT HOME. SHE WORKED ALL THE TIME.

THE DAYS WENT BY, AND ALL OF A SUDDEN, I REALIZED THAT MY MOM ALREADY HAD EVERYTHING SET UP.
I FOUND A LETTER OF RESIGNATION THAT MY MOM PLANNED TO DELIVER IN A FEW DAYS.
I DON'T KNOW HOW SHE DID IT, BUT SHE MANAGED TO GET THE 7,000 BUCKS FOR THE JOURNEY.
MOM, THIS IS FOOLISH. THE THINGS THOSE MEN SAID ARE LIES.
SON, CAN YOU PLEASE STOP?
THE JOURNEY WON'T BE THAT EASY...
I'M FORTY-ONE YEARS OLD AND ALREADY FEELING LIKE AN EIGHTY-YEAR-OLD.
I DON'T EXPECT YOU TO UNDERSTAND,
BUT I'VE ALREADY MADE UP MY MIND.
YOU SEE HOW YOUR DAD WON'T HELP, AND I CAN'T GIVE YOU ALL YOU NEED...
MAYBE THEY'RE LYING, MAYBE IT'LL BE HELL, BUT THAT HELL IS THE ONLY CHANCE I GOT TO SEE SOME LIGHT RIGHT NOW.
MOM...

I COULDN'T SAY ANYTHING. I'D NEVER SPOKEN WITH MY MOM LIKE THAT BEFORE. I REALIZED I WASN'T REALLY AWARE OF EVERYTHING SHE WAS GOING THROUGH.
THEN I REALIZED NOTHING WAS GOING TO STOP HER. I EVEN REMEMBER YOUR MOM TRYING TO TALK HER OUT OF IT, WITHOUT ANY LUCK.

THE NEXT FEW DAYS, I STARTED TO GET REALLY SCARED FOR HER. I COULDN'T IMAGINE HER TRAVELING ALONE. THEN THERE'S ALL THOSE THINGS YOU SEE ON TV—I JUST COULDN'T HELP BUT THINK THE WORST.
AND THAT'S WHEN I DECIDED TO GO WITH HER.
THE ONLY THING THAT MADE MY MOM UNEASY ABOUT LEAVING WAS THE IDEA OF LEAVING ME ON MY OWN. SO IT WASN'T HARD TO CONVINCE HER. EVEN SO, I COULDN'T BELIEVE IT.
NEXT, GILBERTO ASKED FOR ANOTHER 3,000 BUCKS IF I WAS COMING ALONG. MY MOM ONLY HAD TEN DAYS TO GET THE EXTRA MONEY...

BUT SHE DID IT.

I COULDN'T BELIEVE THAT EITHER.

405 SOUTH
San Diego
710 SOUTH
Long Beach

Chapter 2

NO FAREWELLS

THANK GOD IT'S COLD.
THAT MAKES A TRAFFIC JAM MORE BEARABLE THAN THE ONES IN EL SALVADOR. SO HOT AND SWEATY!
WHEN I LEFT HOME, I STILL DIDN'T KNOW HOW TO DRIVE. BUT I SURE DON'T MISS RIDING ON THOSE BUSES.
SO, WHAT HAPPENED THEN?
AFTER AUNT ELENA GOT THE MONEY.
WE COULD GET KILLED, WE COULD GET RAPED... WE COULD DIE IN THE MIDDLE OF THE DESERT, AND NOBODY WOULD FIND US.
I THOUGHT ABOUT WHAT COULD HAPPEN. WHAT WE WERE ABOUT TO DO WAS WAY TOO DANGEROUS.
OR WE COULD MAKE IT BUT WITH NO IDEA WHEN WE COULD EVER COME BACK TO EL SALVADOR.
EVERYTHING HAPPENED SO FAST.
THOSE WERE THE LAST TIMES I'D BE ABLE TO SEE MY LOVED ONES.
THAT'S WHY I DIDN'T SAY GOODBYE TO ALMOST ANYONE... I KNOW YOU UNDERSTAND...
YEAH, MAN.
IN A WAY, I THANK YOU FOR NOT SAYING GOODBYE TO ME.

YOU'RE LIKE A BROTHER TO ME... I DON'T KNOW IF I COULD HAVE HELD BACK MY TEARS.
SEE?
I DIDN'T WANNA REMEMBER ANY SAD FACES.
YOU KNOW?
THE LAST TWO DAYS BEFORE WE LEFT WERE WILD...

2007
I LIKE YOUR PANTS, UNCLE RIGO.
I BOUGHT THEM LAST WEEK AT LAS CHINAMAS.
THEY LOOK REALLY COOL. IT'S HARD TO COME BY PANTS LIKE THAT NOWADAYS.
BLAMM
ACK! ACK!

THEY'RE NICE, RIGHT?
HEY... WHY DON'T YOU SELL THEM TO ME?
NAH! I DON'T THINK SO.
C'MON, DON'T BE LIKE THAT.

I'LL LET YOU KNOW THE NEXT TIME I GO TO LAS CHINAMAS, SO YOU'LL COME WITH ME AND GET YOUR OWN PAIR.
ALL RIGHT, THEN...
CARLITOS!
YEAH!?
ARE YOU SURE YOU DON'T WANT SOME COFFEE?
NO! IT'S OK, MAMA TITA.
I MADE IT WITH A BIT OF CINNAMON, JUST THE WAY YOU LIKE IT.
THANKS, GRANDMA, BUT I HAVE TO GO.
MY LITTLE BROTHER HERE BOUGHT SOME PASTRIES, YOU KNOW?
ARE YOU SURE YOU DON'T WANT SOME?
IT'S GETTING LATE, AND I WANNA DROP BY MY DAD'S.

EVERYTHING OK, SON?
YES, EVERYTHING IS ALL RIGHT, MAMA TITA...
THE BUS IS COMING.
SEE YA!

Libertad
HI, CARLITOS. LOOK HOW YOU'VE GROWN.
HI, MS. BLANQUI.
YOUR DAD IS IN THE OFFICE.
FOR THE MOMENT, I HAVE TO PUT YOU ON THE WAITING LIST, BECAUSE...
SIR, PLEASE...
I CAN'T RESCHEDULE YOUR APPOINTMENT.
WE DON'T HAVE AVAILABILITIES UNTIL TWO WEEKS FROM NOW...

CLACK
CARLOS...
CARLOS...
CARLOS!
SO, WHAT'S GOING ON?
OH... HEY, DAD.
RING
IT'S JUST THAT...
RING
I...
RING RING
I JUST CAME BY...
RING RING
WHAT'S WRONG WITH YOU?
RING
I JUST... I JUST WANTED TO ASK YOU FOR SOME MONEY.
CLICK
BECAUSE I'M LEAVING FOR THE STATES...
CLACK
ARE YOU INSANE? YOU ARE GONNA GET YOURSELF KILLED!

WHEN YOU FIRST TOLD ME, I THOUGHT YOU WERE JUST TRYING TO GET MY ATTENTION.
YOUR MOM IS PUTTING CRAZY IDEAS IN YOUR HEAD.
THINK IT THROUGH...
LOOK, DAD, THIS IS SOMETHING MOM AND I ALREADY DECIDED.
WE'RE LEAVING TOMORROW. I'M NOT SHARING OUR PLANS, BUT... I DON'T EVEN HAVE A NICKEL FOR THE ROAD. IF YOU CAN GIVE ME SOMETHING SO I DON'T GO EMPTY-HANDED... I WON'T BOTHER YOU WITH MONEY ISSUES ANYMORE.
TOMORROW...
PLEASE, DON'T TELL ANY OF THIS TO MAMA TITA AND UNCLE RIGO. THEY'RE GETTING OLD, AND I DON'T WANT THEM TO BE UPSET OR CONCERNED AND...
SIGH
20

I LOVE YOU SO MUCH, SON!
THINK IT THROUGH... YOU SHOULDN'T DO THIS...
CARLOS!!
CARLOS!!

I THINK THIS SHOULD BE ENOUGH.
ACCORDING TO THE COYOTE, IT SHOULD BE LIKE A VACATION TRIP.
STILL, I'M COMING PREPARED.
IF SOMEONE TRIES TO DO ANYTHING TO MY MOM, THIS BLADE IS GOING STRAIGHT TO THEIR THROAT...
NIRVANA
OR...WELL... SOMETHING LIKE THAT.
I MADE A GAP IN MY BELT TO HIDE IT.
I'LL HIDE THE 20 BUCKS MY DAD GAVE ME TOO.
SNIFF
NOBODY WILL THINK TO LOOK HERE!
HEY MAN, DO YOU WANNA GO EAT SOME PUPUSAS?

I WISH I COULD COME WITH YOU. WISH I HAD THE CASH.
WHEN I'M THERE AND MAKING GOOD MONEY, I'LL FIGURE OUT A WAY TO BRING YOU.
WHEN ARE YOU GONNA SAY GOODBYE TO THE GUYS?
HEY, YOU KNOW WHAT... WE SHOULD GO TO MARILYN'S.
THREE WITH CHEESE AND FOUR BEANS WITH CHEESE.
PAT
PAT
PAT
PAT
PAT
PAT
TSSSS
TSSS
DUDE, YOU DEFINITELY GOTTA KISS HER NOW!
NAH, I DON'T WANNA DO THAT. BUT I DO WANT TO SAY GOODBYE TO THE GUYS.
I JUST DON'T WANNA CRY IN FRONT OF EVERYBODY!
I HAVE JUST THE SOLUTION FOR THAT. HANG ON.

ALL RIGHT, THEN. TWO EACH. BOTTOMS UP!
PUPUSERIA MARI
BURP

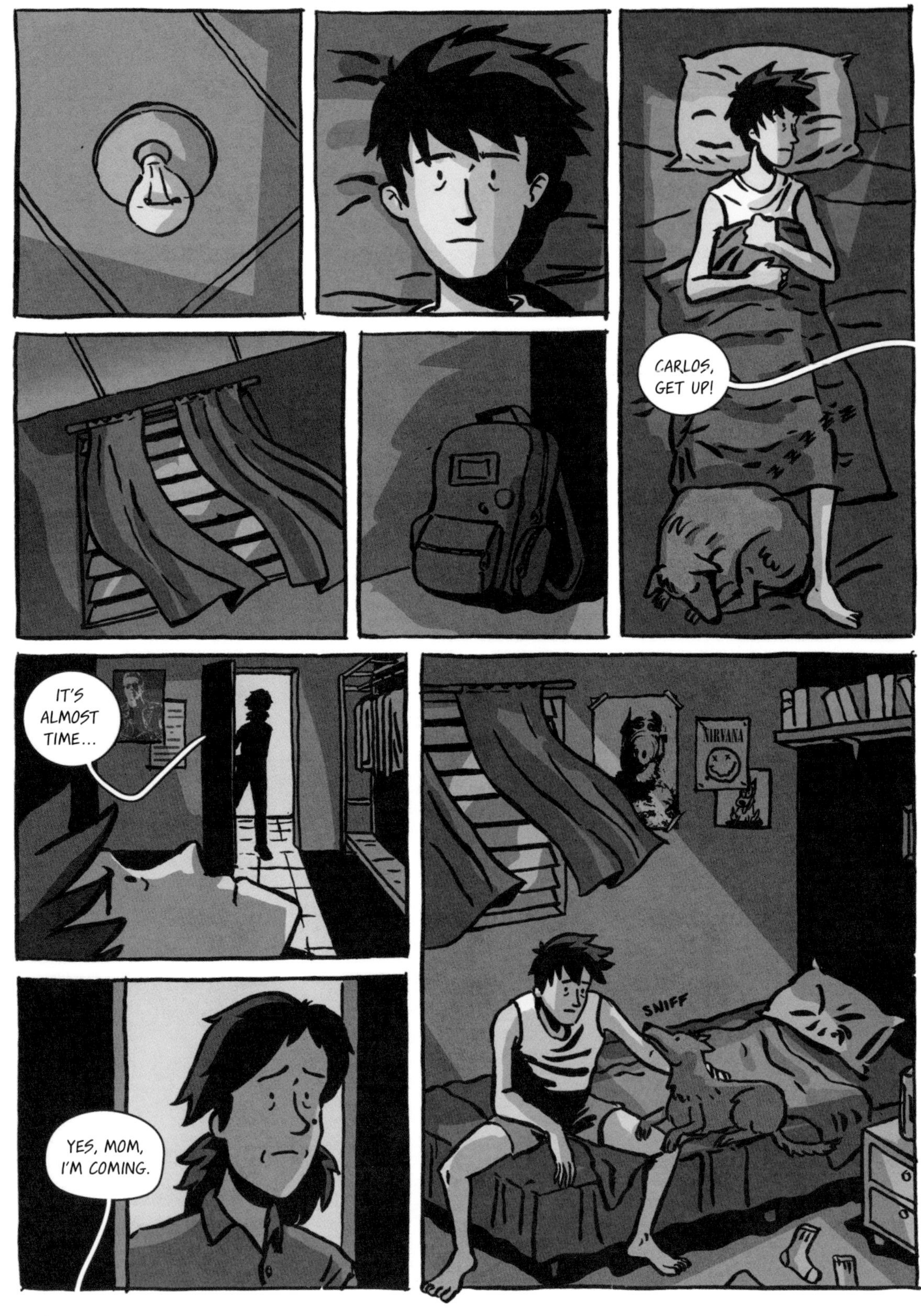
CARLOS, GET UP!
IT'S ALMOST TIME...
NIRVANA
SNIFF
YES, MOM, I'M COMING.

THEY SAID THAT THEY'LL BE HERE AT SEVEN.
5-C
CLICK
5-C
SNIFF
DON'T WORRY. EVERYTHING WILL TURN OUT OK. YOU'LL SEE.

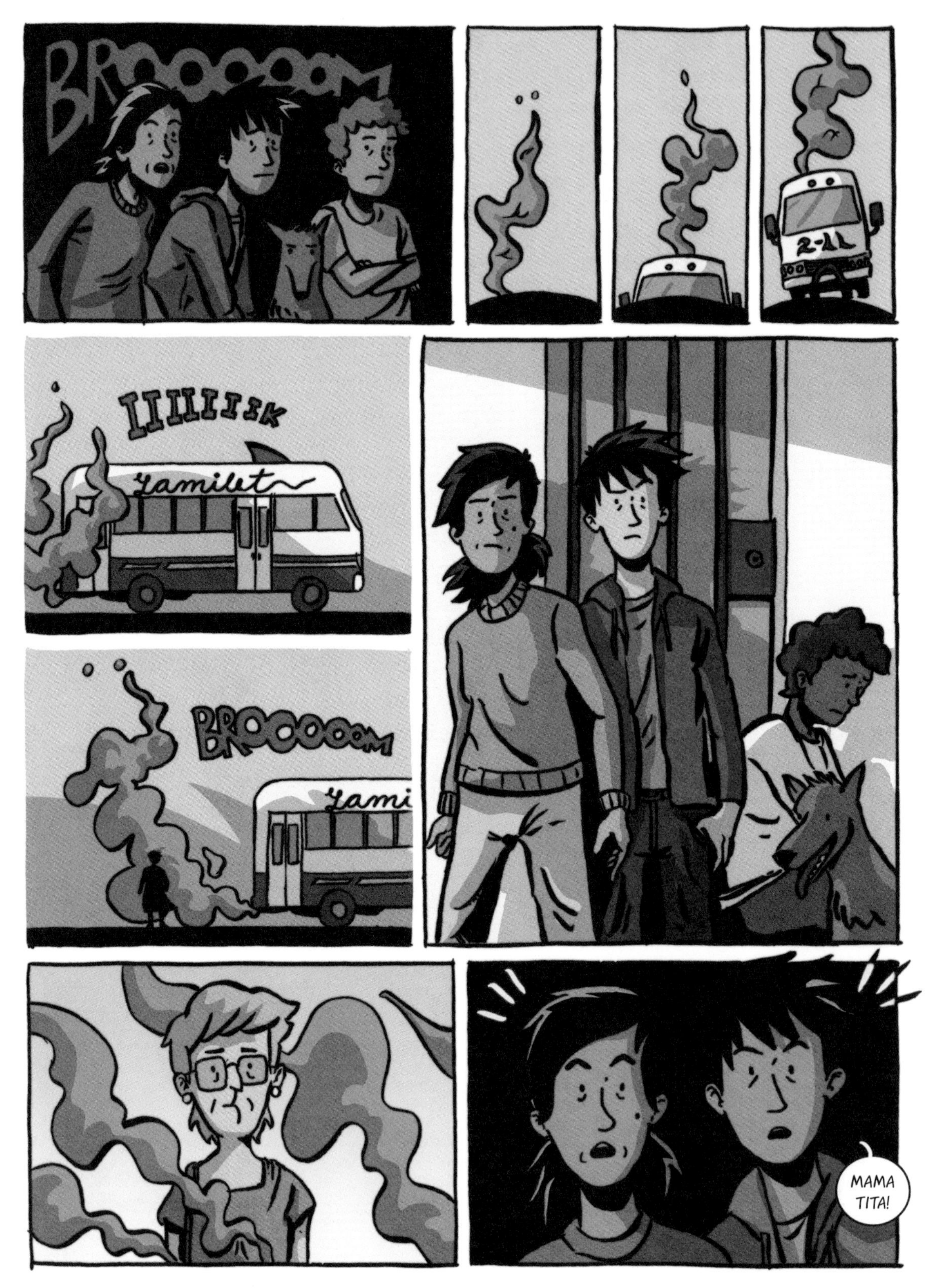
BROOOOOM
IIIIIIIK
Yamilet
BROOOOOM
MAMA TITA!

YOU'D LEAVE WITHOUT TELLING ME? HOW COULD YOU BE SO UNGRATEFUL?
OH, MS. TITA, IT'S JUST THAT WE DIDN'T WANT TO CONCERN YOU AND MR. RIGO.
ENOUGH.
YOU DON'T NEED TO EXPLAIN YOURSELVES... I JUST CAME TO SAY GOODBYE AND...
AND, WELL...
MAMA TITA, I...
LOOK, KIDDO, YOUR UNCLE RIGO SENT YOU THESE.
SIGH

*ALSO KNOWN AS THE HOLY INFANT OF ATOCHA, AN IMAGE OF THE CHRIST CHILD SOMETIMES DISPLAYED BY CATHOLIC PEOPLES OF LATIN AMERICA

THEY'RE HERE...
HI.
ARE YA READY?
I'M GONNA MISS YOU, BOY.
PLEASE TAKE CARE OF HIM...
I'LL MISS YOU, MAN!
WE NEED TO GO!

BE CAREFUL, SON... AND TAKE GOOD CARE OF YOUR MOM.
TAKE A GOOD LOOK AROUND. IT MIGHT BE THE LAST TIME WE'LL SEE ALL OF THIS.

THIS LITTLE PRINT.
I HAVEN'T SEEN MAMA TITA SINCE THEN.
YOU KNOW HOW I LOVE THOSE TWO...
MAMA TITA AND UNCLE RIGO...
Ave 1/2
Ave 1 1/2
107 2 1/4
I EVEN MADE ALL THAT FUSS ABOUT MY UNCLE'S PANTS, JUST TRYING TO MAKE ANOTHER MEMORY OF HIM.
WHEN WE WERE DRIVING AWAY, I COULDN'T LOOK BACK... I WOULD HAVE JUMPED OUT OF THE CAR IF I DID.
YOU REALLY MISS THEM, HUH?
MY MIND WAS SO SCATTERED, THAT WAS THE ONLY THING I COULD THINK OF.
I WISH LIFE WOULD GIVE ME THE CHANCE TO HUG THEM AGAIN.
YOU HAVE NO IDEA WHAT IT'S LIKE TO SEE THE PLACE AND PEOPLE YOU LOVE—AND KNOW IT COULD BE THE FINAL TIME.
SO... 20 DOLLARS?
WHAT A SIGN OF PATERNAL LOVE.
HA, HA, HA.
MAN... YOU HAVEN'T HEARD HALF THE STORY OF THOSE 20 BUCKS.
THERE'S A LONG WAY TO GO.

Chapter 3

JUST ANOTHER STORY

AFTER FOUR HOURS IN THE TRUCK, WE ARRIVED AT THE LAS CHINAMAS BORDER.
DOLLARS TO QUETZALS, QUETZALS TO DOLLARS!
THE OTHER GUY WHO WAS RIDING WITH US DROVE OFF WITH THE CAR.
GILBERTO, OUR "TOUR GUIIDE," STAYED WITH US.
AT FIRST I DIDN'T TRUST HIM... NOT WITH THAT SCARY-LOOKING SCAR HE HAD ON HIS FACE.
THAT'S OUR BUS!
LET'S GO.

THE BUS TOOK US TO GUATEMALA CITY.
THEN WE GOT ON ANOTHER ONE, WHICH TOOK US NEAR TO A TOWN CALLED COATEPEQUE.
THAT'S WHERE THE FIRST SPLAT OF REALITY HIT US.

GILBERTO BROUGHT US TO A HOUSE THAT FELT MORE LIKE A PRISON...
AN AWFUL PLACE. IT WAS A SINGLE ROOM WITH ONE DOOR, NO WINDOWS, A SMALL TV WITHOUT A SIGNAL, AND A FILTHY BATHROOM.
WE STAYED THERE FOR FOUR DAYS WITHOUT STEPPING OUTSIDE, NOT EVEN FOR A LITTLE BIT. NO CHANCE OF SEEING SUNLIGHT, VERY HOT, AND THE FOOD WAS DISGUSTING.
YOU COULD LOSE YOUR SENSE OF TIME THERE. NO WAY OF TELLING NIGHT FROM DAY.
YOU LIED TO US. THIS IS NOTHING LIKE A VACATION...

WE JUST GOT HERE TOO FAST. NOW WE HAVE TO WAIT FOR THE REST OF THE GROUP. TILL THEN, WE STAY INSIDE.
REMEMBER, YOU'RE ILLEGAL HERE.
WE DON'T WANT YOU OUT RUNNING AROUND.
I DON'T KNOW HOW, BUT MY SON AND I AREN'T SPENDING ONE MORE DAY IN THIS DUMP!
FINE, I'LL SEE WHAT I CAN DO. BUT I MAKE NO PROMISES.
I THOUGHT MY PREDICTION WAS GONNA COME TRUE: MY MOM WOULDN'T GET PAST GUATEMALA.
BUT SHE NAGGED SO MUCH THAT, IN THE END, THEY DECIDED TO GET US OUTTA THERE.

WHAT THE HELL ARE YOU DOING?
TAKING NOTES!
WHAT FOR?
I DON'T KNOW...
MAYBE I CAN DO SOMETHING WITH YOUR STORY.
LIKE WHAT? A BOOK?
MAYBE... OR A COMIC BOOK!
YOU'RE TALKING NONSENSE... NOBODY WOULD WANT TO READ ABOUT THIS.
IT'S JUST ANOTHER STORY...
I DON'T KNOW ABOUT THAT, BUT IF YOU DON'T MIND, I'LL KEEP TAKING NOTES.
OH, YOU CAN KEEP WASTING YOUR TIME.
ANYWAY, THEY TOOK US TO A TOWN NAMED NENTÓN, NEXT TO THE BORDER.
THERE, WE GOT TOGETHER WITH A LARGER GROUP OF PEOPLE.
THAT NIGHT, WE WERE GOING TO CROSS INTO MEXICO, HEADING TOWARD CHIAPAS.

THIS IS THE SECOND TIME I'M CROSSING MEXICO TO GET TO THE U.S.
THE FIRST WAS IN 1998. BACK THEN, OVERLAND CROSSING WAS A PIECE OF CAKE.
NOT LIKE NOW.
THAT'S WHY I CAME BACK HERE. SO MY SON WOULDN'T HAVE TO CROSS ALONE.
HOW'D YOU MANAGE TO GET BACK?
EASILY. I CAME BY PLANE!
BACK IN THE STATES, I TURNED MYSELF IN TO LA MIGRA SO THEY WOULD DEPORT ME, AND...
BROOOOOOOM BROOOOMMMMMMM

HURRY! YOU ALREADY KNOW YOUR GROUPS— HURRY!
C'MON! WE'RE NOT MESSING AROUND. RUN!
GODSPEED!

THERE WERE TWELVE PEOPLE INSIDE THE TRUCK.
SEVEN OF THEM WERE SQUEEZED INSIDE THE CARGO BED. UP FRONT WERE MY MOM, GILBERTO, AND ME, ALONG WITH TWO COYOTES.
REMEMBER, IF LA MIGRA GETS US, YOU HAVE TO SAY YOU'RE SAUCEPAN SELLERS.
CLINK
CLINK
"60 PESOS EACH."
DON'T YOU DARE EXPOSE US, FOR ANY REASON.
WE'LL ALL BE SCREWED IF YOU DO.

I FELT LIKE I WAS STUCK IN THERE WITH MY LEGS BENT FOR A THOUSAND HOURS, BUT WE WERE JUST GETTING STARTED.
EVER SINCE THAT TRIP, MY KNEES HAVEN'T BEEN THE SAME.
I DON'T EVEN WANNA THINK ABOUT THE PEOPLE WHO WERE IN THE BACK.
THEY DROVE UNTIL DAWN, ABOUT TWELVE HOURS.

LATER THAT MORNING, WE STOPPED SOMEPLACE SO WE COULD GO TO THE BATHROOM.
I NEVER KNEW WHERE THE HELL WE WERE. ONLY THAT IT WAS SOMEPLACE IN CHIAPAS.
THE TWO COYOTES LEFT WITHOUT AN EXPLANATION, JUST SAID WE HAD TO HIDE. APPARENTLY, THE PEOPLE IN THE AREA DIDN'T LIKE MIGRANTS.
THEY'D CALL THE POLICE EVERY TIME THEY SPOTTED ONE. GOD KNOWS WHY.
DON'T DO THAT.
I CAN'T STAND THE COLD ANYMORE...
YOU MIGHT GET A SNAKE BITE.

CRAK
A CART...
A CART IS COMING!
QUIET. EVERYBODY DOWN.
WHAT'S GOING ON?
MOM, QUIET...
THE HOUNDS WILL NOTICE US.
SNIFF

SNIFF
SOB

THAT'S WEIRD...
HOW NEITHER OF THE DOGS BARKED.
THAT'S WHEN I STARTED TO SEE THINGS. AMAZING, INEXPLICABLE STUFF.
THE COYOTES SHOWED UP THREE HOURS LATER AND BROUGHT US FOOD.
IT WAS SPOILED CHICKEN, BUT WE HAD TO TRY TO KEEP IT DOWN.
WE DIDN'T KNOW THE NEXT TIME WE'D HAVE SOMETHING TO EAT.
I FORCED MYSELF TO FINISH MY SHARE.
REST AREA
I HAVEN'T LIKED CHICKEN EVER SINCE.
I NOTICED A LOT OF STUFF BECAUSE, DURING THE WHOLE RIDE, I COULD HEAR THE COYOTES TALKING.
YOU KNOW WHY THE JOURNEY IS SO EXPENSIVE? BECAUSE, ONCE IN A WHILE, THEY HAVE TO BRIBE THE COPS TO LET THEM THROUGH.

SO THEY DO ANYTHING THEY CAN TO AVOID THOSE BRIBES AND SAVE A LITTLE MONEY.
WHATCHA DOIN'?
WE'RE GOING UP THE HILL SO WE CAN SAVE ON PAYOFFS.
ARE YOU INSANE? LET'S TAKE THE ROAD.
I RATHER DEAL WITH LA MIGRA THAN WITH GUERRILLAS.
IT SOUNDS LIKE YOU DON'T LIKE MONEY.
DON'T BE A CHICKEN!
OUCH!
POW

POW

BANG
GET THE HELL OUT OF THE CAR!
GASP
OUT, YOU BASTARDS.

SHH. DON'T MAKE A SOUND...
YOU KNOW YOU CAN'T HURT US, RIGHT?
DO YOU WANNA BET?!
LISTEN, WE DON'T WANT ANY PROBLEMS.
WHAT IF WE COME TO AN AGREEMENT?

OK, GET IN!
I SAID GET IN!
THAT SCARE YOU? HUH?
I DON'T FIND THIS FUNNY.

DON'T BE AFRAID. WE'RE USED TO BEING MUGGED LIKE THAT.
THE KEY IS TO GIVE THEM A FEW BUCKS SO THEY DON'T KILL YOU IN THE MIDDLE OF NOWHERE.
AND THOSE GUYS ARE HAPPY WITH A FEW BUCKS.
UNLIKE THE COPS.
$
WHAT ABOUT THEM?
HI THERE!

I THINK YOU HAVE SOMETHING FOR ME, MY FRIEND.
WINK
FWEEEEET!
BROOOM
SO LONG, MY LOVE.
SO LONG!

*THE ZAPATISTA NATIONAL LIBERATION ARMY IS A MEXICAN ORGANIZATION THAT FOUGHT FOR THE DEFENSE OF COLLECTIVE AND INDIVIDUAL RIGHTS THAT HAVE BEEN HISTORICALLY DENIED TO MEXICAN INDIGENOUS PEOPLES.

AFTER THAT, WE GOT BACK ON A HIGHWAY, BUT ONLY FOR A WHILE. THEN WE TOOK A PATH THROUGH ANOTHER MOUNTAIN.
THEN, OUT OF NOWHERE, A GROUP OF PEOPLE AT THE VERY TOP OF A MOUNTAIN BEGAN TO SHOOT AT US!
BANG
BANG
UNTIL THE NEXT TIME WE STOPPED, I COULD ONLY WONDER IF ANY OF THE PEOPLE IN THE CARGO BED HAD BEEN SHOT.
BASTARDS!

KEEP YOUR EYES WIDE OPEN. WE'LL PROBABLY SEE A WRAITH.
THEY USUALLY APPEAR IN THESE LANDS.

HEY!

SEE THAT GIRL? I ASKED HER IF SHE COULD TRADE PLACES WITH YOU.

BACK THERE, YOU'LL BE ABLE TO STRETCH YOUR LEGS.

YOU PUT OUR LIVES IN DANGER, AND THAT'S WHAT YOU'RE WORRIED ABOUT?

WHAT DID YOU SAY?
NOTHING, MOM.

SON, IF YOU WANT TO TELL ME SOMETHING, JUST SAY IT.
I DON'T WANT TO TALK RIGHT NOW.

MY MOM JUST WANTED TO HELP, BUT I WAS TOO ANGRY TO REALIZE IT. MY THOUGHTS WEREN'T CLEAR.
THEN, INSIDE THE CARGO BED OF THE TRUCK, I FELT SO COMFORTABLE THAT I DIDN'T THINK ABOUT HER FEELINGS.
WE TRAVELED WITHOUT STOPPING FOR ABOUT THREE MORE DAYS...

Chapter 4

WE ARE AGUSTIN'S PEOPLE

N-OUT
RGER
THESE ARE THE BEST BURGERS YOU'LL EVER TRY.
I PREFER BURRITOS.
I KNOW, BUT THE ONES OVER HERE AREN'T THAT GOOD.
OK, BUT YOU STILL OWE ME A CALIFORNIA BURRITO LATER.
COME ON. THAT'S THE LEAST MEXICAN KIND OF FOOD YOU CAN EAT.
WELL... THIS IS AMERICA!
HOW IS MY AUNT?
SHE'S ALL RIGHT... SHE HAS HER GOOD DAYS AND HER BAD DAYS.
WHY'S THAT?
SHE HAD A LOT OF TROUBLE GETTING USED TO THE WAY OF LIFE AROUND HERE...
SLURP
AND AFTER I GOT MARRIED, IT GOT WORSE. BUT I THINK SHE'S GETTING BETTER...
SO... WHAT HAPPENED AFTER THE THREE-DAY ROAD TRIP?

BY THE END, WE WERE IN VERACRUZ. ALONG WITH GILBERTO, WE SPLIT FROM THE LARGER GROUP. I DON'T KNOW WHAT HAPPENED TO THE OTHERS...
WE WENT TO THIS LITTLE SHACK IN THE MIDDLE OF NOWHERE. A GUY NAMED JUAN WAS WAITING FOR US.
YOU COULD TELL HE AND GILBERTO HAD BEEN WORKING TOGETHER FOR A LONG TIME.
IN THE SHACK, THERE WAS THIS COUPLE AND THREE LITTLE KIDS...
THEY WERE SO POOR THAT THEY DIDN'T HAVE ANYTHING TO EAT.

JUAN WAS GOING TO PAY THEM TO LET US STAY THERE FOR THREE DAYS.
AREN'T YOU GOING TO GIVE TORTILLAS TO THE KIDS?
THE TORTILLAS ARE FOR OUR GUESTS.
NO, IT'S OK... HERE...
CARLOS, THEY'LL BE OFFENDED IF WE DON'T EAT EVERYTHING THEY GAVE US.

BROOO
...MY BOY
JUAN AND GILBERTO ARE HERE FOR YOU.
IT'S TIME TO GO.

WINK

YOU FINISHED?
YEP!
OK, LET'S GO.

WE'RE ALMOST THERE.
SOUTH
5
San Diego

MY MOM IS GONNA BE SO HAPPY. SHE GOT REALLY EXCITED WHEN SHE FOUND OUT YOU WERE COMING.
SHE'S GONNA GET HAPPIER WHEN SHE SEES WHAT MY MOM SENDS HER: TAMALES, PUPUSAS, BEANS...
AND SHE HAD ME PACK POLLO CAMPERO FOR UNCLE EDWIN.

UGH, MY MOM LIKES THAT CHICKEN TOO.
EVEN IF THEY WANTED TO, THEY COULDN'T DENY THAT THEY'RE SIBLINGS.

IF I WERE LIVING OUTSIDE EL SALVADOR, I WOULD MISS THIS CHICKEN TOO.
I HATE CHICKEN!

SO WHERE DID THIS JUAN TAKE YOU?

WE TRAVELED WITH HIM FOR ABOUT TWO DAYS.

HE WAS AN ALL RIGHT GUY. I THINK HE FELL IN LOVE WITH MY MOM, BUT HE NEVER MADE ANY MOVES.

UNITED STATES OF AMERICA
MEXICO
REYNOSA
TAMAULIPAS
TAMPICO
GULF OF MEXICO
PACIFIC OCEAN
POZA RICA
VERACRUZ
CHIAPAS
NENTÓN
GUATEMALA
EL SALVADOR
VERACRUZ IS A VERY LARGE STATE, AND JUAN KEPT MAKING A LOT OF STOPS.
I'D WONDERED IF HE WANTED TO TAKE HIS TIME SO HE COULD KEEP CHECKING IN ON MY MOM... BUT GILBERTO SAID NOTHING, SO I GUESS OUR PACE WAS NORMAL.
GILBERTO IS WEIRD...

WHY DO YOU SAY SO?
HE ALWAYS LOOKS MAD. HE BARELY SPEAKS.
LEAVE HIM ALONE. HE'S FOCUSED ON WHAT HE'S DOING...
AND I DON'T KNOW IF I WANNA HEAR WHAT HE HAS TO SAY.
WHEN WE GET TO THE STATES, I'LL LEARN TO SURF.
OVER MY DEAD BODY.

WHAT'S WRONG WITH SURFING?
JUST SEEING THAT MUCH WATER MAKES ME SHUDDER!
MR. JUAN MAKES ME SHUDDER.
SIGH
I KNOW, RIGHT?! IT SEEMS LIKE IF I GAVE HIM THE SLIGHTEST SIGNAL, HE WOULD PROPOSE TO ME ON THE SPOT.
IF HE ASKS YOU TO MARRY HIM, I WILL GIVE HIM MY BLESSING FOR BEING SO BRAVE.
HE'LL BE YOUR NEW DAD!
HAHAHA
HAHAHAHA

UNITED STATES OF AMERICA
MEXICO
GULF OF MEXICO
REYNOSA
TAMAULIPAS
TAMPICO
POZA RICA
VERACRUZ
CHIAPAS
PACIFIC OCEAN
NENTÓN
GUATEMALA
EL SALVADOR
JUAN TOOK US TO A BUS STATION IN A PLACE CALLED POZA RICA.
CENTRAL DE AUTOBUSES DE POZA RICA
SEÑORA ELENA.
YOU ARE VERY PRETTY...
I WOULD MARRY YOU RIGHT HERE!
OH, DON'T BE SILLY!
ARE YOU CRAZY?
DON'T BE DISRESPECTFUL, MAN!
SMACK

ALL RIGHT, LISTEN TO ME VERY CAREFULLY, BECAUSE THIS WILL DETERMINE IF WE'LL MAKE IT TO THE BORDER ALIVE OR NOT.
FROM HERE ON, YOU KEEP YOUR MOUTH SHUT. YOU CAN'T SPEAK WITH ANYBODY, NOT EVEN TO SAY HI.
IF SOMEBODY ASKS FOR THE TIME, DON'T YOU DARE ANSWER!
WILL PEOPLE TURN US IN TO LA MIGRA, LIKE IN CHIAPAS?
WORSE.
IF THEY HEAR YOUR ACCENT, PEOPLE WILL LET THE NARCOS KNOW.
AND IF THE NARCOS CATCH YOU...
WOULD EVERYONE HERE DO THAT?
NOT EVERYONE. BUT IT'S BETTER NOT TO TAKE ANY RISKS.
THE NARCOS PAY GOOD MONEY FOR THAT INFORMATION. THEY USUALLY ASK RELATIVES OF THE MIGRANTS FOR RANSOM MONEY. OR SOMETIMES THEY USE MIGRANTS AS MULES OR FOR SEX LABOR...
SO, KEEP YOUR MOUTH SHUT.

EXCUSE ME, WHAT TIME IS IT?

UNITED STATES OF AMERICA
MEXICO
REYNOSA
TAMAULIPAS
TAMPICO
GULF OF MEXICO
POZA RICA
VERACRUZ
CHIAPAS
PACIFIC OCEAN
NENTÓN
GUATEMALA
EL SALVADOR

TAMPICO, TAMAULIPAS
C. COLON
ALTAMIRA
CHAMPURRADO
ASADA
TACOS
THERE'S THREE OF US. WE ARRIVE TOMORROW.
WHAT SHOULD WE DO IF THEY STOP US?
OK...

OK.
IF A COP STOPS YOU AND ASKS FOR YOUR PAPERS, DON'T WORRY.
ALL YOU HAVE TO DO IS HAND THEM THIS.
THEN YOU SAY, "WE ARE AGUSTIN'S PEOPLE."
THEY'LL LET YOU GO.
JUST LIKE THAT? ARE YOU SURE?
IF YOU DO EVERYTHING I SAY, THERE'S NOTHING TO WORRY ABOUT.

HEY, GILBERTO, DON'T YOU WANT TACOS?
I'M NOT HUNGRY.
WE ALREADY BOUGHT YOU SOME.
ALL RIGHT... THANK YOU.
SO... HOW DID YOU GET THAT SCAR?
CARLOS!!
YOU DON'T WANNA KNOW...
YES, I DO!!
CARLOS, FOR THE LOVE OF GOD!
IT'S OK, MA'AM. I DON'T MIND.
YOU'VE BEEN FINE, BUT I USUALLY TELL THIS STORY TO GROUPS THAT DON'T TAKE THINGS SERIOUSLY.
OR GROUPS THAT DON'T WANNA LISTEN TO WHAT I SAY.

A FEW YEARS AGO, I WAS...
A DIFFERENT PERSON.
I THOUGHT THIS WAS ALL AN ADVENTURE. JUST A GAME.
I USED TO SET UP MY GROUPS AND THEN TRY TO MAKE THE TRIP ON MY OWN. NO BRIBES, NO OTHER CONTACTS.
I THOUGHT ALL THE BUREAUCRACY WAS UNNECESSARY, AND I COULD SAVE A LOT OF MONEY BY GOING AROUND IT.

MY GROUPS WALKED—A LOT.

WE'D STAY AT OUT-OF-THE-WAY PLACES. I TRIED TO ONLY BRING PEOPLE IN GOOD SHAPE.

I MANAGED TO GET SEVERAL GROUPS TO THE NORTH, NOT REALIZING I HAD BEEN EXTREMELY LUCKY.
GASP
BUT GOOD LUCK RUNS OUT...
ARE YOU THE GUIDE?

YES, THAT'S ME.
WHAT ARE YOU DOING HERE? YOU DON'T KNOW THIS IS A RESTRICTED...
OHH, WAIT A MINUTE...
YOU'RE NO TOUR GUIDE. YOU'RE A COYOTE, AREN'T YOU?

...
YOU BETTER CHOOSE YOUR NEXT WORDS CAREFULLY, SWEETHEART.
I KNOW I SHOULD'VE GIVEN YOU SOMETHING IN ADVANCE... BUT...
CLACK
I CAN MAKE IT UP TO YOU!
CLACK
CLACK
THAT'S WHAT WE WANT TO SEE.
OK, BOYS, BRING ME THE MONEY...
AND GIVE OUR FRIEND A LITTLE LOVE.
POW

YOU JUST AVOIDED A TRAGEDY!
WELL, PEOPLE...
DON'T WORRY...
YOUR GUIDE HAS EVERYTHING COVERED.
EVERYONE WILL WALK AWAY FROM HERE.

OK, PEOPLE!
TIME TO SAY GOODBYE.
BANG BANG BANG BANG
I DON'T KNOW WHY THEY DECIDED TO LEAVE ME ALIVE...

BUT THAT'S HOW CARTEL MEMBERS ARE: RUTHLESS AND UNPREDICTABLE.
AFTERWARD, THEY FORCED ME TO BURY THE BODIES.
WORST OF ALL WAS RETURNING TO EL SALVADOR AND HAVING TO PERSONALLY TELL PEOPLE THAT THEIR RELATIVE HAD DIED.
I'D RATHER DIE MYSELF THAN HAVE TO DO THAT AGAIN.
I KEEP DOING THIS BECAUSE I DON'T KNOW HOW TO DO ANYTHING ELSE.
IT'S GETTING LATE... LET'S GO.

UNITED STATES OF AMERICA
MEXICO
REYNOSA
TAMAULIPAS
TAMPICO
GULF OF MEXICO
POZA RICA
VERACRUZ
CHIAPAS
PACIFIC OCEAN
NENTÓN
GUATEMALA
EL SALVADOR
SCREECH
I.D. NOW.

I'M A MINOR...
AND YOU?
I... LEFT IT AT HOME.
SO?!
WE ARE AGUSTIN'S PEOPLE...
3148

REYNOSA, TAMAULIPAS, BORDER CITY
WITH TEXAS, UNITED STATES

JUST SO YOU'LL HEAR HOW BADASS MY BOSS IS—THIS IS HIS CORRIDO.*

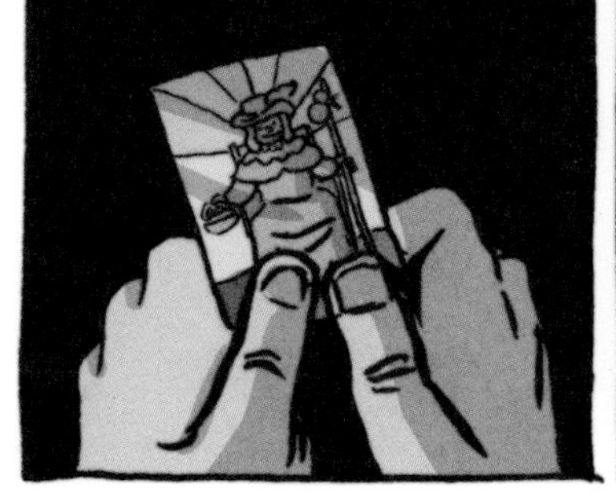

THE SONG TALKED ABOUT THE BOSS'S GREAT DEEDS, HOW KIND AND FAIR HE IS...

GILBERTO'S STORY WAS ECHOING IN MY HEAD THE WHOLE TIME.

*A FORM OF LYRICAL BALLAD

Chapter 5

PELIGRO

*AFFECTIONATE WAY OF CALLING OR NAMING SOMEONE YOUNGER WHO IS ESTEEMED, REGARDLESS OF RELATIONSHIP

WELL, UNCLE EDWIN, HERE'S YOUR CHICKEN.
FINALLY!
POLLO CAMPERO
LET'S SEE... I ALSO BROUGHT EL SALVADOR'S FINEST PUPUSAS, CORN AND MEAT TAMALES, CHEESE...
AND MORE JALAPEÑO TORTILLA CHIPS.
WHY WOULD YOU BRING HIM THOSE?
MY FOOLISH HUSBAND WILL BE COMPLAINING ABOUT A STOMACHACHE ALL NIGHT.
FINE, I WON'T SHARE THEM WITH YOU. YOU'LL BE SORRY ONCE YOU GET HUNGRY, BRENDA!
I'M GONNA MAKE SOME COFFEE.

THESE SWEETS ARE FOR YOU, AUNT MYRA.
THANKS, MY LOVE.
THEY ARE MILK CANES, RIGHT?
OF COURSE.
SNIFF
AND FOR AUNT ELENA, HERE'S SOME MORE CANDIED COCONUT.
THANK YOU, MIJO.
OH, NO. SORRY, SNOOPY.
SNIFF
I DIDN'T BRING ANYTHING FOR YOU.
HA HA HA HA HA HA HA

IN SAN DIEGO, YOU PRACTICALLY WORK JUST TO COVER THE RENT. SO HERE'S WHERE WE LIVE NOW.
HI, POKI. HERE'S MAMA!
CLICK
TWEET TWEET TWEET
TWEET
CLICK
IT'S SMALL, BUT WE'RE SAVING A LOT OF MONEY.
LET'S GO MEET YOUR UNCLE ERNESTO.
COME, I'LL FIX A PLATE WITH JALAPEÑO CHIPS AND CHAMOY.
HEY!
WHAT'S CHAMOY?
IT'S A SAUCE GIVEN BY THE GODS.
AND SOME BEERS IN CASE WE GET THIRSTY.
LET'S GO TO BED, POKI.
GOOD NIGHT, HONEY.
NIGHT, SWEETIE.

YOU THINK YOUR MOM WOULD LIKE TO TALK ABOUT THE... ODYSSEY?
GULP
I DON'T KNOW...
WE NEVER REALLY TALK ABOUT IT OURSELVES. BUT SHE DOES GET VERY ANXIOUS.
I REMEMBER, DURING OUR FIRST DAYS IN THIS COUNTRY, MY MOM WOULD GET REALLY SCARED AROUND LATINO-LOOKING MEN...
YOU MEAN LIKE YOU AND ME?
THE ONES THAT LOOKED LIKE RANCHERS, GUYS FROM THE COUNTRYSIDE, SO TO SPEAK.
WHY'S THAT?
WHAT I'VE TOLD YOU SO FAR IS CLOSEST TO THE VACATION THEY PROMISED TO MY MOM.
REMEMBER HOW SOME DUDE PICKED US UP WHEN WE ARRIVED AT REYNOSA?
SLURP
WELL... HE TOOK US TO A SHELTER.
I THOUGHT WE'D ALREADY PASSED THROUGH THE WORST. BUT I WAS SO WRONG.
WHAT WAS AT THE SHELTER?
THE HOUSE WAS SMALL AND CROWDED...
LIKE 20 PEOPLE THERE, ONLY SALVADORANS, GUATEMALANS, AND HONDURANS. MOSTLY MEN.
I EVEN REMEMBER THAT AMONG THE FEW WOMEN, THERE WAS A PREGNANT LADY.

THE RULES ARE SIMPLE.

JUST DON'T MAKE NOISE, AND BE MINDFUL OF OTHER PEOPLE'S BELONGINGS.
I RECOMMEND THAT YOU DON'T LEAVE YOUR THINGS UNATTENDED, SO WE AVOID FIGHTS.
THE MEN SLEEP HERE ON THE FLOOR. WOMEN ARE IN THE ROOM OVER THERE.

LIGHTS-OUT AT SEVEN.

WE EAT TWICE A DAY.
IF YOU WANT TO USE THE BATHROOM, YOU HAVE TO LET ME KNOW FIRST.
YOU'LL LEARN THE REST OF THE RULES SOON.
COME IN.
I'M ANGELICA, BY THE WAY.
YOU'LL GO THE REST OF THE WAY WITHOUT ME.
BUT I ASSURE YOU YOU'RE IN GOOD HANDS. I'VE ALREADY TAKEN CARE OF EVERYTHING.
I DON'T KNOW HOW MANY DAYS YOU'LL HAVE TO WAIT HERE, BUT WHEN IT'S YOUR TURN TO CROSS THE BORDER, I'LL COME TO SEE THAT EVERYTHING'S ALL RIGHT.
IS THAT CLEAR?
THANKS FOR EVERYTHING, GILBERTO.
WELL... YOU COMING OR NOT?

TOOOT
TOOOUOT
TOOOUT
TOOOOT
WHY SO QUIET?
IF YOU WANT TO TELL ME SOMETHING, NOW IS A GOOD TIME.
I HEARD WE'LL HAVE TO SWIM ACROSS THE RIO BRAVO.
DON'T SAY THAT. GILBERTO SAID WE WEREN'T EVEN GOING TO SEE THAT RIVER.

SON, I LOVE YOU. I NEVER WANTED TO PUT YOU IN DANGER...
OF COURSE NOT. BUT WHAT DID YOU THINK WOULD HAPPEN?
THAT I WAS GOING TO LET YOU COME ALONE?
WITHOUT ME, YOU WOULDN'T HAVE EVEN MADE IT THROUGH GUATEMALA.
AND YEAH, I AM ANGRY. BECAUSE OF YOU, I LEFT BEHIND EVERYTHING I LOVE...
SON...
I DON'T WANNA TALK ANYMORE...
SIGH.....
I LOVE YOU TOO, MOM...
WHAT TIME IS IT?
AROUND SIX O'CLOCK.
EVERYBODY GOES TO BED SO EARLY HERE.
I THOUGHT THE LIGHTS WENT OFF AT SEVEN.
MA'AM.
I'LL SHOW YOU WHERE YOU'LL SLEEP.

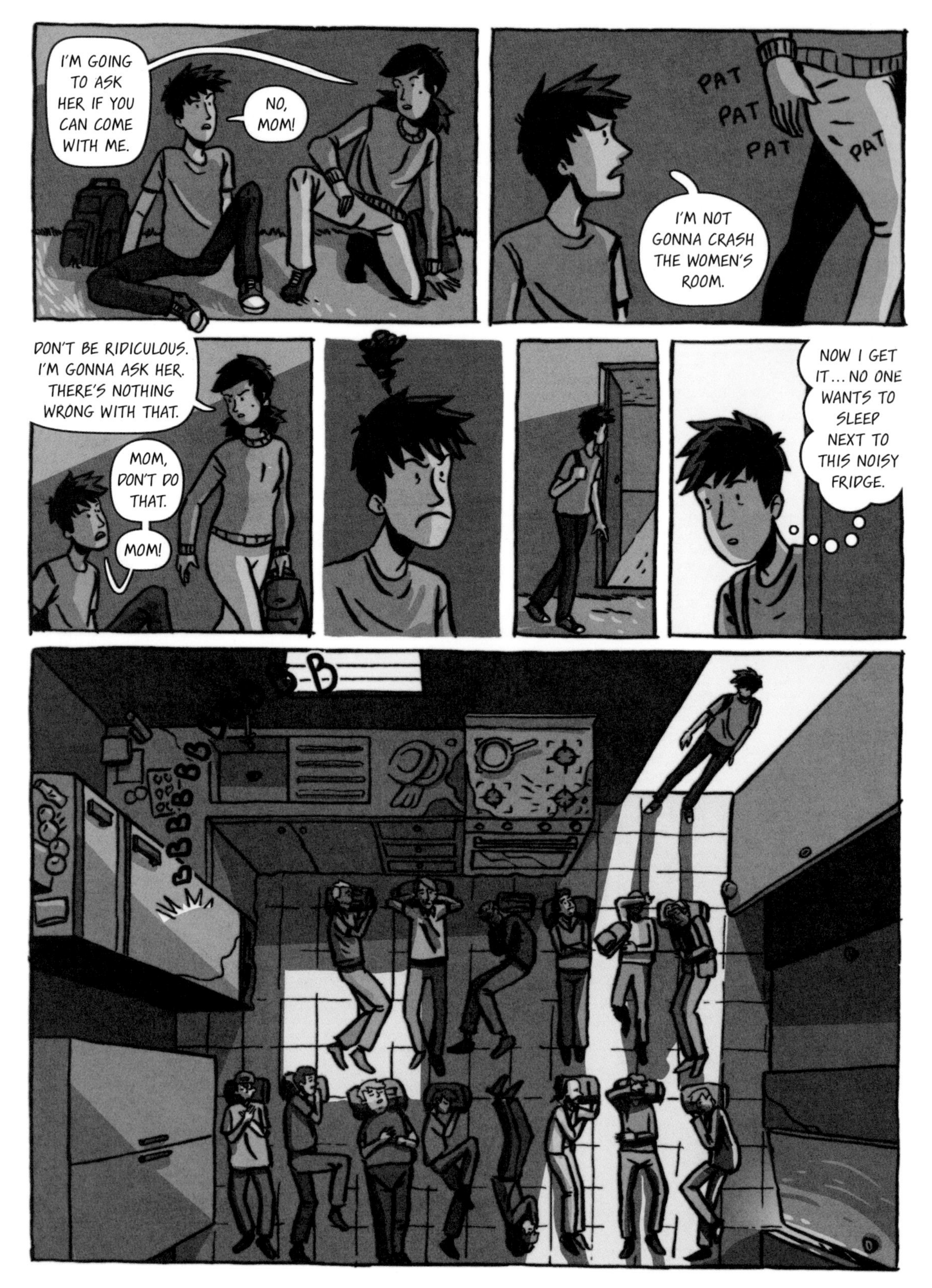

I'M GOING TO ASK HER IF YOU CAN COME WITH ME.
NO, MOM!
PAT PAT PAT PAT
I'M NOT GONNA CRASH THE WOMEN'S ROOM.
DON'T BE RIDICULOUS. I'M GONNA ASK HER. THERE'S NOTHING WRONG WITH THAT.
MOM, DON'T DO THAT.
MOM!
NOW I GET IT... NO ONE WANTS TO SLEEP NEXT TO THIS NOISY FRIDGE.
B-B-B-B-B-B
MMM

WHAT'S THAT FOR?
YOUR EARS.
WHY?
IS EVERYONE HERE A BIG SNORER OR WHAT?
NO... LOOK BEHIND YOU.

YOU GOTTA BE KIDDING ME!
HEY... CAN WE SLEEP INSIDE THAT ROOM?
YOU CAN... BUT I WOULDN'T.

CARLOS...
CARLOS!
COME. COME LIE HERE.
NO, MOM. THEY'LL NOTICE I'M BEING TREATED DIFFERENTLY.
DON'T BE RIDICULOUS!
ANGELICA SAID YOU COULD.
BBBBBB

WHY WON'T YOU TALK TO HIM?
HUSH, HE'LL HEAR YOU.
CUT IT OUT!
I COULD ASK HIM TO COME SLEEP NEXT TO YOU.

WE SPENT SIX DAYS IN THAT SHELTER, BUT IT DIDN'T TAKE ME LONG TO GET INTO THE ROUTINE.
THE FIRST THING WE DID, AFTER WE WOKE UP, WAS HAVE BREAKFAST. THEN WE HAD TO TAKE TURNS USING THE SHOWER.
AND AFTER THAT, YOU HAD... NOTHING LEFT TO DO.
WINK
EVERY DAY, WE HAD TO FIND SOME WAY TO ENTERTAIN OURSELVES.
EVERYBODY USED TO GO TO THE BACKYARD AND TALK.
FROM THAT, I LEARNED THE STORIES OF SOME OF THE PEOPLE THERE.
THERE WAS A LADY FROM HONDURAS WITH HER FOURTEEN-YEAR-OLD DAUGHTER.
THE PREGNANT WOMAN WAS FROM HONDURAS TOO. SHE HAD BEEN AT THE SHELTER FOR THREE MONTHS ALREADY.
SHE HAD RUN OUT OF MONEY AND WAS WAITING FOR SOMEONE TO SEND HER MORE, SO SHE COULD REUNITE WITH HER HUSBAND IN HOUSTON.

SOME OF THE MEN IN THE BACKYARD WERE TALKING ABOUT HOW WE ALL GOT TO WHERE WE WERE. SOME TALKED ABOUT HOW THEY GOT MUGGED ON THEIR WAY NORTH. OTHERS SAID THEY WERE ALMOST KILLED.

*DANGER

BELIEVE IT OR NOT, I'M A TOUGH BONE TO DRILL.
MY BROTHER KNOWS I'M NOT LYING. HE WOULDN'T LET ME!
ISN'T THAT RIGHT, CHALIO?
YEAH, BRO...
WE CAME ALL THE WAY HERE ON OUR OWN!
I WOULDN'T HAVE TAKEN THIS SHOT WITH ANYONE OTHER THAN MY BROTHER!
WE KNOW HOW TO SURVIVE BECAUSE WE BOTH FOUGHT IN THE SALVADORAN WAR.
ISN'T THAT RIGHT, CHALIO?
YEAH, BRO.
I WAS PART OF THE ATLACATL BATTALION.
WE SAW COMBAT. THE WORST OF THE WORST.

SINCE I WAS FEARLESS... EVERYONE STARTED CALLING ME PELIGRO.

WE WERE SURROUNDED BY GUERRILLAS, AND WE HAD TO HOLD THE SIEGE SEVERAL DAYS. NO FOOD OR WATER.

BECAUSE OF THE TERRAIN, A RESCUE BY MOTOR VEHICLE WAS IMPOSSIBLE. AND BY AIR, IT WAS WAY TOO DANGEROUS, BECAUSE THEY COULD SHOOT RPGS AT THE HELICOPTERS.

FROM TIME TO TIME, A HELICOPTER WOULD FLY BY QUICK TO DROP PROVISIONS BOXES TO US.
OH LORD, FINALLY!
AND WHENEVER ONE OF THOSE BOXES FELL...
KEEP YOUR HEAD...
BANG
THE CARNAGE STARTED!
BOOM
FIRE!!!

BANG
BANG
PAW
PAW
PAW
PAW
POW
PAW
BANG
FFFFFFFFF
BOOM

GASP
CRACK
HUMPH
CHALIO?!
BRO!!!

SORRY I CAN'T GIVE YOU THE WHOLE BOX.
REINFORCEMENTS ARE COMING!
RUN AWAY, BROTHER! THIS IS GONNA GET UGLY.
HUF HUF
HUF HUF
WE SPENT NEARLY FIVE DAYS IN THOSE TRENCHES.
THE BATTLE I MENTIONED WAS FOR THE LOST BOX.
BEFORE, THE OTHERS MANAGED TO TAKE SOME BOXES. BUT MY SIDE TOOK IT THAT DAY.
FINALLY, THE REINFORCEMENTS ARRIVED AND TOOK US OUTTA THERE. THEN THE HIGH COMMAND SENT US HOME.
I WAS IN BAD SHAPE. I HAD TO SLEEP WITH MY RIFLE BETWEEN MY ARMS. AND WHENEVER I HEARD A WEIRD NOISE, I WOULD EMPTY THE LOADER, SHOOTING EVERYWHERE.
I BECAME KINDA... INSANE.
THANK GOODNESS I NEVER KILLED ANYONE FROM MY FAMILY.

WITH TIME, AND SOME ELECTROSHOCK THERAPY, I GOT BETTER...
I WAS A BRAND-NEW MAN.
ISN'T THAT RIGHT, CHALIO?
YEAH, BRO!
DID YOU HAVE TO RETURN TO COMBAT AFTER THAT?
OH, NO. AFTER THAT, EVERYONE THERE WAS DISCHARGED.
I CAME BACK TO MY HOMETOWN AND BECAME A FISHERMAN. THAT'S WHEN CHALIO AND I REUNITED, AND WE BECAME PARTNERS.
WE HAD GOOD YEARS AND BAD YEARS, BUT THE LAST ONE WAS THE WORST.
THE DAY CHALIO AND I DECIDED TO LEAVE EL SALVADOR, WE HAD WORKED FROM FOUR IN THE MORNING UNTIL SIX IN THE EVENING, AND WE ONLY MANAGED TO MAKE SIX BUCKS, WHICH WE SPLIT.
THREE BUCKS FOR FOURTEEN HOURS OF WORK...

I THINK GETTING ON THE ROOF OF THAT TRAIN WAS THE WORST PART OF OUR JOURNEY. SOME PEOPLE THERE FELL OFF WHILE THEY WERE SLEEPING.

WE PASSED THROUGH PLACES WHERE KIDS WOULD THROW ROCKS OR FILTHY WATER AT US. BUT ALSO, THERE WERE PLACES WHERE SOME WOMEN THREW US FOOD AND CLEAN CLOTHES.

*THE BEAST

ONE DAY, TWO GANG MEMBERS GOT ON THE TRAIN.
THEY SEEMED PRETTY CONCERNED.
I ASKED THEM WHAT WAS WRONG. THEY TOLD ME THEY'D SCREWED UP A JOB.
SOB
SOB

IN MEXICO AND OTHER PARTS OF LATIN AMERICA, THE APPEARANCE OF A BLACK BUTTERFLY ANNOUNCES THE DEATH OF A LOVED ONE OR IS CONSIDERED A SYMBOL OF BAD LUCK.

Chapter 6
STAY

AFTER PELIGRO FINISHED TALKING, NOBODY WANTED TO SHARE THEIR STORY.
NOBODY BELIEVED THEY HAD ONE THAT COULD COMPARE.
PELIGRO (CRAZY EYES DUDE)
SCARS LEFTSIDE
SURVIVED A SHOOTING?
CIVIL WAR IN EL SALVADOR
BUT FINALLY, EACH PERSON SPOKE.
MOST OF THEM LEFT THEIR HOMES DUE TO LACK OF WORK. OTHERS WERE FLEEING FROM GANGS. OTHERS WERE TRYING TO REJOIN THEIR FAMILIES IN THE STATES.
NOBODY WAS IN THAT SHELTER JUST BECAUSE.
THAT JOURNEY WAS THEIR LAST HOPE...
THEIR ONLY BEAM OF LIGHT.

NO ONE DARED TO DO IT, BUT I THINK IT WAS BECAUSE NOBODY WANTED TO SPEAK DIRECTLY TO THAT MAN.

HUF
HUF
HUF

GILBERTO SAID WE WOULDN'T HAVE TO CROSS THE RIVER. I THOUGHT THEY WERE TAKING US DOWN A DIFFERENT PATH.
MOM, STOP THINKING ABOUT IT...
SIGH
IF WE HAVE TO CROSS THAT RIVER, WE'RE BETTER OFF TURNING BACK!
IF YOU WANT, YOU CAN TURN BACK ON YOUR OWN. I'M GOING ALL THE WAY TO THE END.
I WON'T ALLOW YOU TO SET ONE FOOT IN THAT RIVER...
I'M NOT EVEN HUNGRY. I MIGHT TRY TO SLEEP FOR A BIT.
BON APPÉTIT.
MERCI, MADEMOISELLE.
YOU SPEAK FRENCH?!
NOT REALLY. THOSE ARE THE ONLY WORDS I KNOW.
YOU'RE FULL OF SURPRISES, HANDSOME...

MY MOM WAS TERRIFIED BY THE IDEA OF CROSSING THE RIVER. ONE TIME, YEARS EARLIER, SHE ALMOST DROWNED IN THE SEA.
I KNEW SHE'D BEEN TRAUMATIZED BY IT... BUT I DIDN'T COME TO TALK TO HER.
?
outside
11PM
SOB
SOB
SOB
SOB
SNIF
I JUST IGNORED HER... I DON'T KNOW WHY. I DIDN'T MANAGE THE WHOLE SITUATION PROPERLY.
SOB
SNIFF

YOU REALIZE THOSE THINGS WITH TIME.
YOU SHOULDN'T STILL FEEL GUILTY BECAUSE OF IT.
AT AGE 19, MOST OF US BEHAVE LIKE IDIOTS.
YEAH... YOU'RE PROBABLY RIGHT.
OK... LET'S GET BACK ON TRACK. YOU WENT TO SEE ANGELICA THAT NIGHT, RIGHT?
HA HA HA.
WHAT ELSE COULD I DO?

CREEEAK
CREEEAK
HEY, HANDSOME.
WHY SO NERVOUS?
I DIDN'T SEE YOU BACK THERE.
YOU'RE LEAVING TOMORROW.
REALLY?!
YOU KNOW, I DON'T WORK FOR THAT MAN.
I'M JUST COVERING FOR A FRIEND WHO'S ON VACATION.
I DON'T LIKE THE JOB, BUT IT IS WHAT IT IS.
WELL... YOU'RE JUST HELPING YOUR FRIEND.

LOOK.
I LIKE YOU...
...AND WE DON'T HAVE MUCH TIME.
OH...
I WANT YOU TO STAY WITH ME.
I MAKE DECENT MONEY. I EVEN HAVE MY OWN HOUSE.
I COULD GET YOU A JOB.
OR, IF YOU WANT, YOU COULD STUDY HERE IN MEXICO. I CAN PAY FOR EVERYTHING.
JUST STAY...
FIRST OF ALL... THANKS. I THINK.
BUT I CAN'T ACCEPT THAT. I CAN'T LEAVE MY MOM.
SHE CAN STAY TOO!
SORRY... WE CAN'T.

THIS IS MY NUMBER.
GULP
WHEN YOU GET TO YOUR FAMILY, I WANT YOU TO CALL ME.
I CAN MEET YOU WHEREVER YOU ARE. I CAN COME TO AND FROM THE STATES AS I PLEASE. BUT CALL ME!
OK… I'LL CALL YOU.
AND I WANNA GIVE YOU THIS.
AFTER YOU'VE CROSSED THE RIVER, RUB THIS GARLIC ON YOUR SHOES AND PANTS.
WHY?
COME CLOSER.
IT'LL SCARE AWAY THE SNAKES, AND THE DOGS WON'T SMELL YOU.
THANK YOU, ANGE…

CARLOS, YOU NAUGHTY DOG!
HEY! I DIDN'T DO ANYTHING...
EH... I'M GONNA MAKE SOME COFFEE.
WANT SOME?
YES, PLEASE.
SO, DID YOU LEAVE THE NEXT DAY?
YES. GILBERTO CAME TO SORTA SAY GOODBYE.
WELL... THIS IS IT.
YOU'LL BE WITH YOUR FAMILY IN THE BLINK OF AN EYE. YOU'LL SEE.
MY MOM DIDN'T SAY ANYTHING. SHE FELT CHEATED BECAUSE OF THE RIVER... FOR SOME REASON, I FELT LIKE I SHOULD HUG HIM, BUT I HELD BACK.
HE WAS A VERY TORMENTED GUY.
WE NEVER HEARD FROM HIM AGAIN.

IT'LL BE READY IN A MINUTE.
CLICK
AROUND 5:00 P.M., TWO MEN CAME AND PULLED A GROUP TOGETHER.
THERE WERE NINE OF US IN TOTAL.
WE HURRIED INTO A VAN WITH NO SEATS.
WE DIDN'T GET THE CHANCE TO SAY GOODBYE TO ANYBODY.
EVERYTHING WILL BE OK. OLD LADIES HAVE CROSSED, AND YOU'RE STILL YOUNG.
WE'RE GOING TO GET THROUGH. THEY KNOW WHAT THEY'RE DOING.
CARLOS... IT'S NOT WORTH IT. WE BETTER HEAD BACK.
LISTEN, MOM. IF YOU WANT TO GO BACK, GO FOR IT. I'LL CONTINUE.
IT'S PAINFUL TO SAY ALL THIS OUT LOUD.

WHAT THE HELL WAS GOING THROUGH MY MIND, TO TREAT MY MOM LIKE THAT?
HAVE YOU EVER TALKED ABOUT IT WITH HER?
LIKE I SAID, WE DON'T TALK ABOUT THE TRIP AT ALL, NEVER MIND THOSE ARGUMENTS.
AND FOR ME, IT'S EMBARRASSING TO REMEMBER HOW I BEHAVED WITH HER... BUT I GUESS I HAVE TO ACCEPT THAT IT HAPPENED.
I THINK I'LL HAVE TO CHARGE YOU SOON FOR THIS THERAPY SESSION.
I HAD DECIDED TO TAKE THE TRIP WITH MY MOM TO LOOK AFTER HER... THAT WAS ALWAYS TRUE. BUT AT THE SAME TIME, I WAS VERY ANGRY.
I BELIEVED THAT EVERYTHING BAD HAPPENING TO US WAS HER FAULT.
AND SEEING HER COMPLICATE THINGS INFURIATED ME.
WHEN YOU'RE A CHILD, YOU NEVER THINK THAT YOU'LL SEE ONE OF YOUR PARENTS PANIC.
THAT NIGHT, ON THE SHORE OF THAT RIVER, I LOST THAT PART OF MY INNOCENCE.

HUFF
HUFF
HUFF

IF YOU WANT TO MAKE IT ACROSS ALIVE, YOU HAVE TO DO EVERYTHING WE SAY. NO COMPLAINTS.
WHEN WE REACH THE RIVERBANK, MAYBE I'LL TELL YOU TO GET DOWN ON THE GROUND.
YOU BETTER HIT THE GROUND—FAST!
KEEP YOUR EYES SHUT THE WHOLE TIME. DON'T YOU DARE OPEN YOUR EYES.
PEOPLE PATROLLING THE RIVER USE NIGHT-VISION GOGGLES. EYE SHINE CAN GIVE YOU AWAY.
NOW, I DON'T WANT ANY BRAVE ONES. THIS RIVER LOOKS CALM, BUT IT HAS STRONG CURRENTS.
EVEN EXPERIENCED SWIMMERS COULD DROWN.
BOTTOM LINE: YOU ALL DO AS WE SAY!
NOW, LET'S GO...

TAKE OFF ALL YOUR CLOTHES AND PUT THEM IN THE PLASTIC BAGS.
YOU AND YOU, HELP US INFLATE THE FLOATS.

ALL RIGHT!

ONCE AGAIN, YOU TWO, THE BETTER SWIMMERS, WILL BE IN BACK, PUSHING.

THE WOMEN WILL GO ON TOP WITH ALL THE STUFF.

THE REST WILL HOLD THE FLOATERS TOGETHER.
C'MON!

HUF
HUF
HUF
HUF
HUF
I WON'T GO! PLEASE, I CAN'T!
EASY, MOM.
CARLOS, LET'S GO! I CAN'T... I CAN'T.
QUIET! YOU—BE QUIET!
PLEASE, I CAN'T... I WON'T GO...
SHUT HER UP!
OR ELSE!

CALM HER DOWN, OR WE'RE GONNA LEAVE YOU BEHIND!
MOM...
EVERYTHING WILL BE OK...
EVERYTHING WILL BE OK.
PELIGRO...
YES, MA'AM?
IF SOMETHING HAPPENS TO ME... LOOK AFTER MY SON.
NOTHING WILL HAPPEN TO YOU, MA'AM... BUT I WILL TAKE CARE OF HIM, AND I WILL TAKE CARE OF YOU TOO.
I PROMISE, I WON'T LET ANYTHING HAPPEN TO YOU.

EVERYBODY DOWN!
ALL CLEAR. LET'S GO.

BEFORE GOING INTO THE WATER, I WAS PRETTY CONFIDENT, BUT WHEN I FELT THE CURRENT, I GOT REALLY SCARED. I'VE HARDLY EVER FELT FEAR LIKE THAT.

I THOUGHT THAT I WAS LOOKING AFTER MY MOM.

THAT'S WHEN I REALIZED THAT HAVING MY MOM BY MY SIDE WAS GIVING ME STRENGTH.
WITHOUT HER, I WOULDN'T HAVE MADE IT THAT FAR...
MY ANGER WAS GONE.

Chapter 7

THE JUMP

I TRIED TO HELP EVERYBODY AS MUCH AS I COULD, BUT IT WAS SO HARD.

MOM, COME HERE.
IT'S GARLIC.
YOU HAVE TO RUB THIS ON YOUR SHOES...
WHICH ONE OF YOU HAS GARLIC?!
YOU BROUGHT IT. THAT'S GOOD.
GIVE SOME TO THE OTHERS, AND RUB IT ON YOUR SHOES AND PANTS.
READY?
ALL RIGHT. THE RULES ARE SIMPLE.
DON'T GO NEAR THE BUSHES, KEEP UP, AND REMEMBER, ALWAYS DO AS WE SAY.

OUCH!
MOM, ARE YOU OK?
I'M FINE...
LET'S GO.

I DON'T KNOW WHERE WE GOT THE STRENGTH TO WALK SO MUCH.
IN ALL THAT TIME, WE HAD NOTHING TO EAT, NOT A DROP OF WATER.
I WAS A BUNDLE OF PAIN...
WALKING DURING THE DAY WAS HORRIBLE. THE HEAT MADE ME WISH FOR NIGHTFALL.

BUT WHEN IT GOT DARK, I FELT ANGRY AT THE NIGHT FOR TAKING SO LONG TO ARRIVE.
POLICIA
WOOF
WOOF
WOOF
WOOF
WOOF

TO CLIMB THAT HILL, YOU NEED TO RUN AS FAST AS YOU CAN SO YOU DON'T COME ROLLING BACK DOWN.
PANT
PANT
HUF
HUF
HUF
I'LL STAY BACK TO HELP MY MOM.
NO, YOU GO UP FIRST AND HELP HER FROM THE TOP.
OK... HEAD UP!

POOF
OUCH!
DON'T WORRY, KID. WE'VE BEEN THROUGH THIS BEFORE.

OK, MOM.
JUST ONE MORE TIME...

PSSST

ALONG THE WAY, THERE WERE VERY NARROW STREETS THAT WOULD CROSS LONG SECTIONS OF THE DESERT.

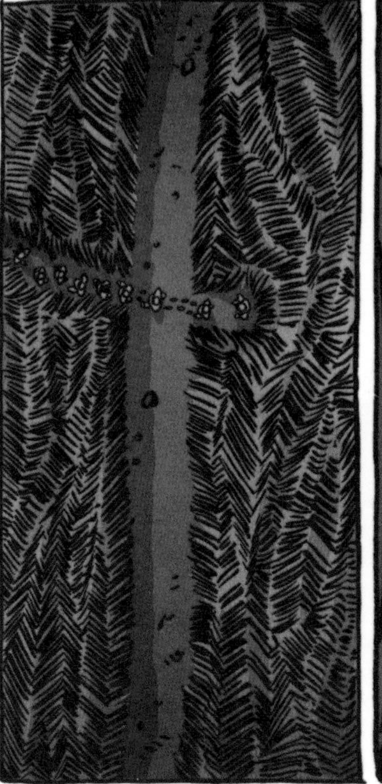

OK, TIME TO REST.
OH MY GOD, WATER!!
SLURP
SLURP
EEW! THIS TASTES LIKE SHIT!
PUAJ
BARF
HUUK
IKK

I DON'T WANT TO DRINK FROM THERE!
YOU HAVE TO, HONEY. WE DON'T KNOW WHEN WE'LL GET WATER AGAIN.

POFF
SOB
JUST A LITTLE FARTHER...

FINALLY, WE SAW IT.
THE AMERICAN DREAM, LYING AHEAD BEHIND A WIRE FENCE!
I WAS SO TIRED, I DIDN'T EVEN GET EXCITED. I JUST WANTED IT ALL TO END.

ONCE YOU REACH THE OTHER SIDE, YOU ALL HAVE TO RUN AS LOW TO THE GROUND AS POSSIBLE.
ONCE YOU GET TO THOSE BUSHES, STAY CROUCHED DOWN.
YOU WILL LIE THERE UNTIL YOU SEE MY SIGNAL. I DON'T WANNA SEE ANY HEADS UP.
THAT'S WHERE WE WAIT FOR THE TRUCKS TO PICK US UP.
MY MOM'S ANKLE ISN'T GOOD. SHE WON'T BE ABLE TO CLIMB. LEMME STAY BACK TO...
NO, YOU GO. WE'LL HELP HER.
I WANT TO HELP HER!
KID, DON'T BE STUBBORN.
HAVEN'T WE TOLD YOU? IT'S OUR WAY OR THE HIGHWAY.
ONE MORE COMPLAINT AND WE'LL LEAVE YOU BOTH HERE.

CALM DOWN, SON. I CAN DO IT.
WHAT IF YOU CAN'T? WHAT IF YOU FALL?!
IF SOMETHING HAPPENS TO ME, YOU HAVE TO KEEP GOING AND DON'T LOOK BACK.
MOM, I WOULD NEVER...
ALL RIGHT, LET'S DO IT.

HUMPF
SIGH
HOP

C'MON,
MOM...
C'MON...
HAAAAAAAA

WHEN I SAW MY MOM FALLING,
I FELT LIKE I WAS DYING.
GASP!
CAN YOU IMAGINE? SEEING YOUR MOM DROP FROM THAT HIGH...
I COULDN'T HOLD BACK— I CRAWLED OVER TO HER.
ONCE WE WERE TOGETHER... ALL THE FATIGUE IN THE WORLD HIT ME... AND I FELL ASLEEP.

SIGH
I GUESS THE ADRENALINE HAD BEEN KEEPING YOU ON YOUR FEET.
HOW LONG DID YOU SLEEP?
I DON'T KNOW.
I FELT LIKE IT DIDN'T LAST LONGER THAN THE BLINK OF AN EYE.

EVERYBODY UP!
HURRY, PEOPLE!
THE WOMEN GO IN FRONT!

WELCOME TO AMERICA!
FLOP

SEE?
IT WASN'T THAT HARD.
SMILE. YOU'RE IN AMERICA NOW!
WE CROSSED. THEY ALL MADE IT.
WHO?
YES, BOSS.
YOU TWO. THE BOY AND THE LADY.
YES, YOU TWO.
COME HERE.

WHAT'S HAPPENING?
YOU PAID FOR THE VIP TREATMENT.
TIME TO GO!
CAN WE AT LEAST SAY GOODBYE TO THE OTHERS?
WHAT FOR?
HEY, MAN, WE JUST WANNA SAY BYE!
AND I JUST WANT YOU TO SHUT YOUR MOUTH!
THERE IS NO TIME FOR THIS SHIT.
AS YOU CAN IMAGINE, WE DIDN'T HAVE A CHOICE BUT TO COMPLY.
BROOOOOM
LEAVING WITHOUT SAYING GOODBYE LEFT A VOID INSIDE ME... THAT WAS THE LAST TIME I SAW PELIGRO AND THE OTHERS.

Chapter 8
CONSUELO

Z Z Z Z Z Z Z Z Z Z Z Z Z Z
WAKE UP, SLEEPYHEADS.
POW
WHAT DID YOU TWO TALK ABOUT LAST NIGHT?
CARLOS WAS TELLING ME WHAT HE WENT THROUGH TO COME HERE.
THE WHOLE STORY?
ALMOST... I'M JUST MISSING ONE PART.
OH... I THOUGHT THAT WAS THE END!
I WISH.
THEY TOOK US TO A HOUSE IN SOME RUN-DOWN NEIGHBORHOOD.
LATER, I LEARNED WE WERE IN A PLACE CALLED MCALLEN, TEXAS.
SLURP
ONCE WE WERE IN THE HOUSE, THEY LOCKED US INSIDE A ROOM.
AT FIRST, WE THOUGHT THAT THEY WERE HIDING US. BUT WE WERE WRONG.

FIRST, THEY TOOK AWAY ALL OUR STUFF.
THEN, THEY LET US SHOWER AND GAVE US CLEAN CLOTHES.
SIGH
BECAUSE THE PANTS I GOT WERE TOO BIG FOR ME, THEY LET ME KEEP MY BELT.
I ALSO GOT TO KEEP THE SANTO NIÑO DE ATOCHA PRINT MAMA TITA GAVE ME.
HAHA
HAHA
HAHAHA
HA

THIS ALL SEEMS STRANGE...
MAYBE WE'RE WAITING ON ANOTHER GROUP?
I DON'T KNOW. THESE MEN ARE MAKING ME NERVOUS.
DID YOU HEAR THAT? EVERYONE SHUT UP.
CLICK
CLANK
HERE, IT'S YOUR BROTHER.
IT'S ON SPEAKER.
HELLO?
ELENA, THANK GOD.

THESE PEOPLE DON'T WANT TO LET YOU GO. THEY'RE ASKING ME FOR TEN THOUSAND DOLLARS...
GASP
BUT WE ALREADY PAID FOR EVERYTHING.
I KNOW... I TRIED TO SPEAK WITH GILBERTO, BUT HE'S NOWHERE TO BE FOUND.
LISTEN TO ME—I HAVE A FRIEND THAT MIGHT BE ABLE TO HELP US.
YOU JUST HANG ON AND TRY TO KEEP...
NOW YOU KNOW WHAT'S GOING ON.
PRAY THAT YOUR BROTHER SENDS US THE MONEY.
SLAM

CONSUELO WAS THE CLEANING LADY.
IN THE FOUR DAYS WE'D BEEN LOCKED UP, WE COULD SEE THAT SHE WAS A GOOD PERSON.
SHE WAS ALWAYS KIND TO US, AND THE TRUTH IS, SHE GAVE US GOOD VIBES FROM THE BEGINNING.
CLICK
HI. TIME TO EAT.
THANK YOU, CONSUELO!
IS SOMETHING GOING ON? EVERYBODY SEEMS PRETTY SHAKEN.
THE BOSS'S GODSON IS COMING.
CONSUELO, COULD YOU... COULD YOU MAYBE GET US A PHONE?
OH, MA'AM, I DON'T HAVE A PHONE...
THEY LEND ME ONE SOMETIMES TO SPEAK WITH MY DAUGHTER IN HONDURAS. BUT THEY'RE ALWAYS KEEPING AN EYE ON ME.
THE THING IS...
I'M THEIR PRISONER TOO. JUST LIKE YOU... I'VE ALREADY BEEN HERE THREE YEARS...

HEY!
YOU! GET LOST, GODDAMMIT.
YES, BOSS!
MY SISTER CALLED ME YESTERDAY. WORRIED.
SHE SAID SHE THINKS YOUR BROTHER IS UP TO SOMETHING AND SHE DIDN'T WANNA BE HERE ANYMORE.
BUT SHE TENDS TO GET A LITTLE PARANOID. KNOW WHAT I MEAN?
NOW, MY GODFATHER, HE LOVES ME DEARLY…
HE LOVES ME SO MUCH HE HAS ME DOING THIS KINDA "ADMINISTRATIVE" WORK.
I DON'T REALLY LIKE IT. I WANNA BE ON THE FRONT LINES, BRINGING PEOPLE OVER.
BUT IT IS WHAT IT IS… YOU KNOW WHO MY GODFATHER IS, RIGHT?
TSK
TSK
TSK
HE'S THE MAN. HE'S BOUGHT OUT ALL OF REYNOSA.
THIRTY GRAND A MONTH TO THE COPS, ANOTHER FIFTY GRAND TO OUR… PARTNERS.
"WE ARE AGUSTIN'S PEOPLE." SO NOBODY CROSSES US.

MY SISTER DOESN'T SEEM TO GET THAT.
I'M SURE YOU DO.
I JUST SPOKE WITH YOUR BROTHER...
HE SAYS HE HAS THE MONEY AND THAT HE'LL COME AROUND HERE TO GIVE IT TO US.
AND IF HE DOESN'T COME THROUGH...
TWEET
WE COULD MAYBE SEND SOME FINGERS OF YOURS TO MAKE HIM COME TO HIS SENSES.

WHAT HAPPENED NEXT? DID UNCLE EDWIN FOLLOW ALONG?
DO YOU REMEMBER HOW UNCLE SAID HE HAD A "FRIEND"?
WELL, YEARS AGO, HE MET THIS GUY AT CHURCH. HE WAS A COP.
A WHILE LATER, THE MAN WAS TRANSFERRED TO TEXAS, AND HE KEPT CLIMBING UNTIL HE SWUNG A JOB AT THE FBI.
FBI?!
CLINK
CLANK
YEAH. WHAT REALLY HAPPENED—AND I FOUND OUT ABOUT THIS LATER—IS THAT MY UNCLE ASKED HIM FOR HELP SO THEY COULD GET US OUTTA THERE.
THE MAN AGREED, AND FROM THAT MOMENT, HE WAS THE ONE THAT GOT IN TOUCH WITH THEM, PRETENDING TO BE MY UNCLE.
HUH! NO WONDER SHE DIDN'T TRUST HIM...
YEAH, HE COULD SPEAK PERFECT SPANISH, BUT HE WAS AMERICAN, HE DIDN'T HAVE AN ACCENT...
SSSSSS
THAT NIGHT, THANKS TO CONSUELO, WE WERE ABLE TO TALK WITH HIM.

YOU TWO!
GULP
COME WITH ME.
EVERYONE ELSE BE READY FOR ORDERS.
I DON'T WANNA HEAR THAT THE RADIOS AREN'T PICKING UP SIGNALS OR SHIT LIKE THAT.
WELL, IMMA GO TO THE BACKYARD. THIS PIECE OF JUNK ONLY WORKS THERE.
TELL THIS FOOL TO STOP SCREWING AROUND.
GULP
GULP
GULP
ALL RIGHT, COLORADO, YOU BUM, STOP DRINKING AND GET UP.
BRO... I'M WASTED...
C'MON, YOU DON'T WANNA GET YOUR BALLS CUT OFF.

THE KID IS TAKING TOO LONG.
MOM!
DUDE, IF HE HEARD YOU CALLING HIM THAT, HE'D CUT YOUR BALLS OFF.
SHHHH
WHATEVER, MAN... WHATCHA THINK IS HAPPENING?
MOM!!
DUNNO, BUT HE SAID TO WAIT FOR ORDERS...
MOM!!!
WHAT?!
CLANK

CLICK
HERE. SPEAK... QUICK.
I THINK THEY WANNA DO SOMETHING TO YOU!
BIP
BIP
BIP
HELLO? EDWIN?
ELENA... THANK GOODNESS. I'M GONNA HANG UP.
BUT...
WHAT HAPPENED?
HE HUNG UP ON ME...
C'MON... IF THEY SEE US, THEY'LL KILL ME!

BBBBB
LISTEN CLOSELY. WE JUST CAUGHT TWO OF THE KIDNAPPERS.
EDWIN... IS THAT YOU?
NO, I'M A FRIEND OF YOUR BROTHER. I WANNA HELP YOU.
YOU HAVE TO FIND A WAY OUT OF THERE BY ANY MEANS.
WHEN THE OTHERS FIND OUT WHAT WE DID, THEY'LL GIVE THE ORDER TO KILL YOU BOTH.
CARLOS, WE HAVE TO ESCAPE!
ARE YOU NUTS? THEY'LL KILL US...
WE NEED A PLAN AT LEAST.
NO, RIGHT NOW, RIGHT THIS SECOND. LET'S GO!

COME! QUICKLY!
MOM... IF THEY SEE US, THEY'LL—
SON, TRUST ME, WE HAVE TO GO!

CONSUELO!
CONSUELO, COME WITH US...
I CAN'T...
MY DAUGHTER.
CLICK

HUF
HOF
HUF
HUFF
HUF

OVER THERE, THAT STORE
K-Store
SCREEEEEE
BROOM
MAYBE THEY CAN HELP...
HEY!
COME HERE...
GET IN!
CALM DOWN. I WON'T HURT YOU. MY NAME'S LUIS.
HUF
CLICK
HUF
HUF
HUF
HUF
DON'T WORRY ABOUT HIM. I KNOW HE LOOKS SKETCHY, BUT HE'S MY FRIEND.

YOU'RE GONNA BE FINE HERE. WE WON'T OPEN THE DOOR FOR ANYONE.
IRON LION ZION
FROM THE MOMENT I SAW YOU, I KNEW YOU GUYS NEEDED HELP. EVERYONE AROUND HERE KNOWS THE GUYS IN THAT HOUSE AREN'T IN AN HONEST LINE OF WORK.
DO YOU NEED SOMETHING?
DO YOU HAVE A PHONE?
I DO, BUT I DON'T HAVE ANY CREDIT...
IF YOU HAVE MONEY, I CAN GO BUY SOME.
CLINK
CLINK
CLINK

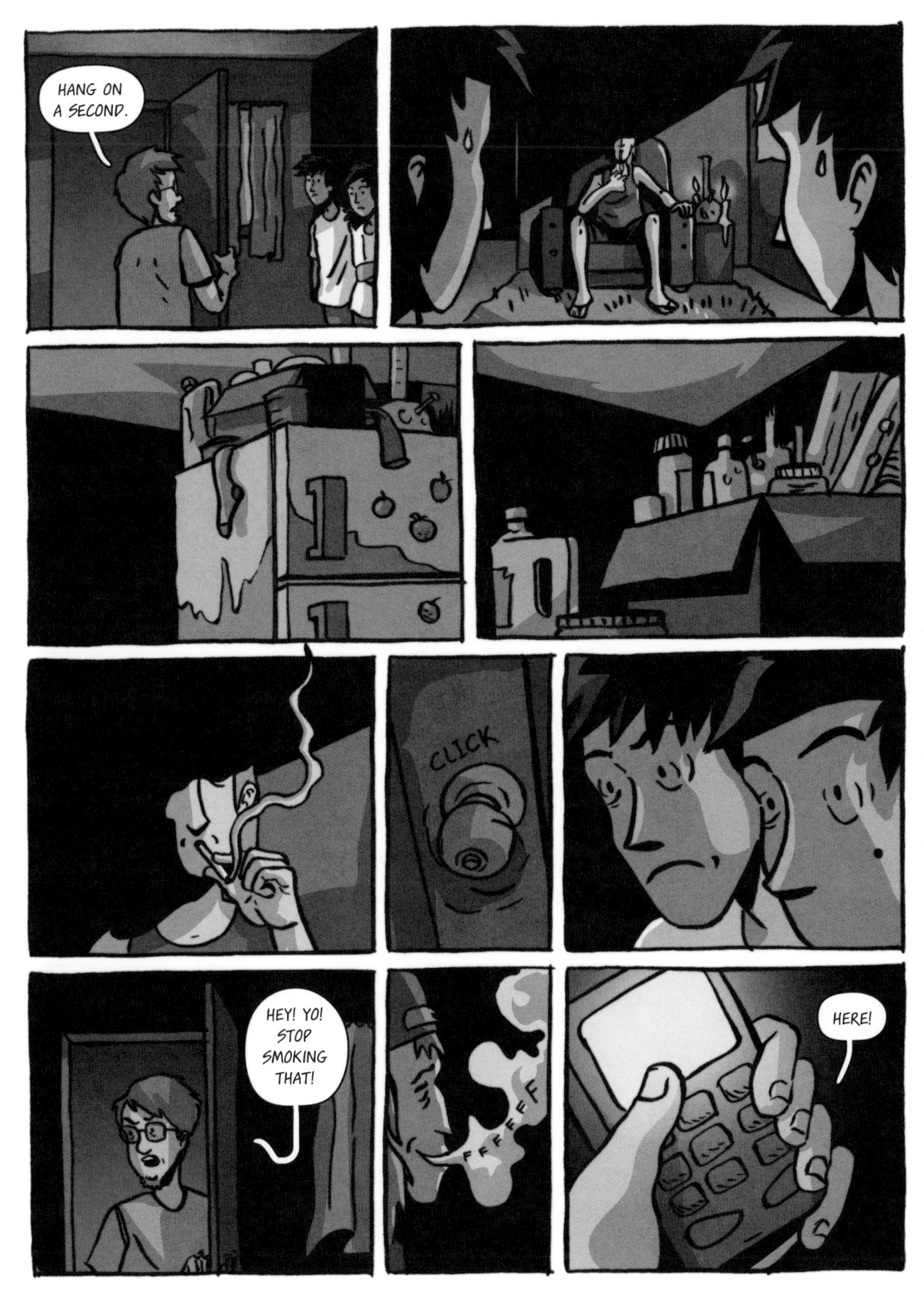
HANG ON A SECOND.
CLICK
HEY! YO! STOP SMOKING THAT!
FFFFFF
HERE!

UNCLE, IT'S ME...
I DON'T KNOW...
HANG ON...
GIVE HIM THE ADDRESS TO THIS HOUSE, PLEASE.
QUEENS AVENUE, 785...
...
HE HUNG UP.
TSK
BBBBB
HELLO?
CARLOS, IS THAT YOU?
YES...

THIS IS BRYAN. I'M YOUR UNCLE'S FRIEND. I'M FROM THE FBI.
WE HAVE YOUR LOCATION. WAIT THERE AND DON'T GO OUT FOR ANY REASON.
THEY SAY THEY'RE COMING FOR US... THE FBI...
FBI!
HI HI HI
I HEAR SOMETHING.
GO HIDE.

BANG
BANG
CRAK
SLAM
NOBODY MOVE!

COME ON, DON'T BE SCARED... I'M BRYAN.

Chapter 9
ELENA

THEY ASKED US ABOUT FIVE TIMES IF LUIS AND THE STONER WERE THE COYOTES.
AT THE END, WE MANAGED TO CONVINCE THEM THE GUYS WERE JUST HELPING US.
WE NEVER KNEW WHAT BECAME OF THOSE TWO. I HOPE THE AGENTS LET THEM GO HOME...
THEN WE WERE ABLE TO GUIDE THE AGENTS TO THE HOUSE WHERE THEY'D HELD US.
I WAS AFRAID TO TELL THEM, AFTER EVERYTHING AGUSTIN'S PEOPLE HAD SAID ABOUT THEIR BOSS... BUT WE THOUGHT THAT MAYBE THE AGENTS COULD HELP CONSUELO.
WE WERE TOO LATE. THE HOUSE WAS ALREADY DESERTED, AND THEY HAD TAKEN CONSUELO WITH THEM.
I HOPE SHE'S OK, WHEREVER SHE IS.

THAT NIGHT, WE SLEPT IN A HOTEL.
THEY GAVE US MONEY TO GET FOOD OR BUY SOME CLOTHES, BUT WE WERE SO SCARED THAT WE DIDN'T GO OUT.
THE NEXT DAY, THEY TOOK US TO A POLICE STATION.
AGENTS TOOK OUR FINGERPRINTS AND ALL OUR INFORMATION.
THEN THEY QUESTIONED US FOR HOURS.
THAT SAME DAY, THEY GAVE US A PERMIT TO TRAVEL FREELY ACROSS THE UNITED STATES.
LAST, THEY TOOK US TO A BUS STATION, AND WITHOUT TOO MUCH FUSS, WE LEFT.
THIRTY-THREE HOURS LATER, WE REUNITED WITH UNCLE EDWIN IN SAN DIEGO...

SOMETIME LATER, THEY GRANTED US A "U VISA."
THAT'S FOR VICTIMS WHO HAVE BEEN ABUSED BY CRIMINALS AND THEN HELP THE AUTHORITIES TO ARREST THOSE CRIMINALS.
A COUPLE OF YEARS LATER, WE APPLIED TO BE PERMANENT RESIDENTS. BUT WE'RE STILL WAITING FOR THE RESOLUTION OF THAT.
SO WE CAN'T LEAVE THE COUNTRY...
SOMEWHERE IN THERE, TEN YEARS PASSED BY.

AND SO IT GOES...

I ALWAYS COME WITH CARLOS WHEN HE'S SURFING.
I LIKE TO TAKE LONG WALKS ON THE BEACH.
I WOULD TOO. I LIKE THIS WEATHER.
ALTHOUGH THE COLD SAND BETWEEN MY TOES FEELS WEIRD.
I PREFER THE WARM SAND OF EL SALVADOR.
I REALLY MISS IT THERE... BUT THE IMMIGRATION PROCESSES ARE SO COMPLICATED...
KNOWING WE CAN'T LEAVE THIS COUNTRY UNTIL WE HAVE GREEN CARDS MAKES ME FEEL TRAPPED.
ABOUT A YEAR AGO, DURING ONE OF MY WALKS, I FOUND A SEA LION.

IT'S COMMON TO SPOT SEA LIONS OVER HERE, BUT NOTHING LIKE THAT ONE.
HE WAS JUST THERE, WATCHING THE HORIZON. HE SEEMED SO SAD. EVERY BREATH WAS LIKE A LONG SIGH OF LONGING.
I'M NOT PRETENDING TO TELL YOU I KNEW WHAT WAS GOING ON INSIDE IT...
BUT I COULD SEE MY OWN FEELINGS REFLECTED.
THIS COUNTRY IS QUITE COLD. IN MANY WAYS, WE'RE BETTER OFF HERE, BUT SOMETIMES I FEEL SO ALONE... LIKE THAT SEA LION MIGHT HAVE FELT.
I CAME BACK THE NEXT DAY, HOPING TO FIND IT THERE AGAIN.
IT WAS A FOOLISH IDEA, BUT IN THAT MOMENT, I HAD THOUGHT WE'D FORMED SOME KIND OF BOND.
CRASH.

SOMETIMES I THINK ABOUT WHAT WOULD HAPPEN IF I GO BACK...
YOU SHOULDN'T.
OVER THERE, EVERYTHING GETS HARDER. EVERY DAY.
I KNOW THAT... BUT I'M TERRIFIED BY THE IDEA OF NEVER SEEING IT AGAIN.
I THINK IT'S A FEAR EVERYONE IN THIS SITUATION FACES.
IT'S COMMON TO SEE US STARING AT THE HORIZON.
A CLOUD OR A TREE.
OLD PICTURES.
LISTENING TO THE CHIRP OF A BIRD OR TO CUMBIA THAT REMINDS YOU OF NEW YEAR'S PARTIES...

PEOPLE TELL ME THAT GOING BACK WOULD BE LIKE ADMITTING I MADE A MISTAKE...
SOME KIND OF FAILURE.
BUT I DON'T SEE IT THAT WAY.
MY SON IS DOING WELL. HE HAS A BRIGHT FUTURE AHEAD OF HIM.
I BELIEVE I ALREADY ACCOMPLISHED SOMETHING...
AND I'M NOT GOING TO APOLOGIZE, NOR FEEL SHAME FOR TRYING TO FIND MY OWN HAPPINESS.
MAYBE THAT SEA LION WASN'T SAD.
MAYBE IT WAS SATISFIED WITH WHAT IT HAD DONE IN ITS LIFE. MAYBE IT HAD FINISHED A LONG JOURNEY.
MAYBE HE WAS GETTING READY TO GO BACK HOME...

TITA...

HEY, CARLITOS!
EAT THIS EGG.
EAT THAT? NO WAY!
THIS IS PURE VITAMINS.
SLURP

IT'S LATE, AND IT'S FREEZING OUT THERE.
WHERE WERE YOU?
YOU NEED SOME WARM CLOTHES...
CARLITOS! COME HERE, MY BOY.

DID I EVER TELL YOU THE STORY OF WHEN MY DAD CAME FACE-TO-FACE WITH A GHOST?

I WAS JUST A KID...

1923–2020

Acknowledgments

To my parents, for their unconditional love and support.

To Francia, Martín, and Miguel, for being there when I needed them most.

To Nicolas, for believing in my work.

To Greg and Athena, for helping me bring this book to life.

To Cesar, for trusting me with his story.

About the Author

Ernesto Saade is an El Salvador-born architect turned cartoonist. After years spent in the world of construction, in 2016, he left to pursue his master's degree in illustration and comics from the Elisava Barcelona School of Design and Engineering. In 2018, he began his new career, writing and drawing several comics based on real-life events and published by nongovernmental organizations. He is now a freelancer who spends 100 percent of his time drawing. Find him at instagram.com/saadernesto.